SADDLE GALS

A Filmography of Female Players in B-Westerns of the Sound Era

by

Steve Turn

&

Edgar M. Wyatt

Foreword by

Jennifer Holt

Published by

Empire Publishing, Inc.
Box 717
Madison, NC 27025-0717
(910) 427-5850

Other Western movie books published by Empire Publishing, Inc:

The Roy Rogers Reference-Trivia-Scrapbook Book by David Rothel
The Gene Autry Reference-Trivia-Scrapbook Book by David Rothel
More Cowboy Shooting Stars by John A. Rutherford and Richard B. Smith, III
Allan "Rocky" Lane, Republic's Action Ace by Chuck Thornton and David Rothel
Tom Mix Highlights by Andy Woytowich
An Ambush of Ghosts by David Rothel
Tim Holt by David Rothel
Whatever Happened to Randolph Scott? by C. H. Scott
Randolph Scott / A Film Biography by Jefferson Brim Crow, III

Empire Publishing, Inc.
Box 717
Madison, NC 27025-0717
(910) 427-5850

Library of Congress Catalog Number 94-62172
ISBN Number 0-944019-19-6

Published and printed in the United States of America

1 2 3 4 5 6 7 8 9 0

COVER ART by Patrick Downey

CONTENTS

___HERITAGE OF THE DESERT .... PAR ..... 1932 ..... RANDOLPH SCOTT
___WILD HORSE MESA .... PAR ..... 1932 ..... RANDOLPH SCOTT
___FIGHTING MAD .... MON .... 1939 ..... JAMES NEWILL

BETTY BLYTHE

___WESTERN COURAGE .... COL ..... 1935 ..... KEN MAYNARD
___DAWN ON THE GREAT DIVIDE ...... MON .... 1942 ..... BUCK JONES
___BAR TWENTY .... UA .... 1943 ..... WILLIAM BOYD

VIRGINIA TRUE BOARDMAN

___BRAND OF HATE .... SUP ..... 1935 ..... BOB STEELE
___BRAND OF THE OUTLAWS .... SUP ..... 1936 ..... BOB STEELE
___THE FUGITIVE SHERIFF .... CLY ...... 1936 ..... KEN MAYNARD

ADRIAN BOOTH

___RED RIVER RANGE .... REP ..... 1938 ..... WAYNE/CORRIGAN
___THE STRANGER FROM TEXAS ..... COL ..... 1939 ..... CHARLES STARRETT
___BULLETS FOR RUSTLERS .... COL ..... 1940 ..... CHARLES STARRETT
___RIDING DOWN THE CANYON .... REP ..... 1942 ..... ROY ROGERS
___ROARING RANGERS .... COL ..... 1946 ..... CHARLES STARRETT
___HOME ON THE RANGE .... REP ..... 1946 ..... MONTE HALE
___MAN FROM RAINBOW VALLEY ..... REP ..... 1946 ..... MONTE HALE
___OUT CALIFORNIA WAY .... REP ..... 1946 ..... MONTE HALE
___LAST FRONTIER UPRISING .... REP ..... 1947 ..... MONTE HALE
___ALONG THE OREGON TRAIL .... REP ..... 1947 ..... MONTE HALE
___UNDER COLORADO SKIES .... REP ..... 1947 ..... MONTE HALE
___CALIFORNIA FIREBRAND .... REP ..... 1948 ..... MONTE HALE
___GALLANT LEGION .... REP ..... 1948 ..... BILL ELLIOT
___THE PLUNDERERS .... REP ..... 1948 ..... ROD CAMERON
___TIMBER TRAIL .... REP ..... 1948 ..... MONTE HALE
___THE LAST BANDIT .... REP ..... 1949 ..... BILL ELLIOTT
___BRIMSTONE .... REP ..... 1949 ..... ROD CAMERON
___ROCK ISLAND TRAIL .... REP ..... 1950 ..... FORREST TUCKER
___THE SAVAGE HORDE .... REP ..... 1950 ..... BILL ELLIOTT
___OH! SUSANNA .... REP ..... 1951 ..... ROD CAMERON

RENE BORDEN (RENEE)

___RIDIN' LAW .... B4 .... 1930 ..... JACK PERRIN
___CANYON HAWKS .... B4 .... 1930 ..... YAKIMA CANUTT
___FIGHTING HERO .... REL ...... 1934 ..... TOM TYLER
___KID COURAGEOUS .... SUP ..... 1935 ..... BOB STEELE
___WESTERN JUSTICE .... SUP ..... 1935 ..... BOB STEELE

VEDA ANN BORG

___THE LAW COMES TO TEXAS .... COL ..... 1939 ..... BILL ELLIOTT

___MELODY RANCH .... REP ..... 1940 ..... GENE AUTRY
___ARKANSAS JUDGE .... REP ..... 1941 ..... ROY ROGERS
___MARKED TRAILS .... MON .... 1944 ..... STEELE/GIBSON
___RIDER FROM TUCSON .... RKO ..... 1950 ..... TIM HOLT
___BITTER CREEK .... AA .... 1954 ..... BILL ELLIOTT

GENEE BOUTELL

___THE FIGHTING COWBOY .... SPR ..... 1933 ..... BUFFALO BILL, JR.
___LIGHTNING RANGE .... SPR ..... 1934 ..... BUDDY ROOSEVELT
___RAWHIDE ROMANCE .... SPR ..... 1934 ..... BUFFALO BILL, JR.
___THE WHIRLWIND RIDER .... AME ..... 1935 ..... BUFFALO BILL, JR.

MARLA BRATTON

___WEST OF THE LAW .... IMP ...... 1934 ..... WALLY WALES
___THE WAY OF THE WEST .... SPR ..... 1934 ..... WALLY WALES
___THE LONE RIDER .... IMP ...... 1934 ..... WALLY WALES
___TIMBER TERRORS .... S&S ..... 1935 ..... JOHN PRESTON

EVELYN BRENT

___HOME ON THE RANGE .... PAR ..... 1935 ..... RANDOLPH SCOTT
___SONG OF THE TRAIL .... AMB ..... 1936 ..... KERMIT MAYNARD
___HOPALONG CASSIDY RETURNS .. PAR ..... 1936 ..... WILLIAM BOYD
___SUDDEN BILL DORN .... UNI .... 1937 ..... BUCK JONES
___THE LAW WEST OF TOMBSTONE RKO ..... 1938 ..... HARRY CAREY
___WIDE OPEN TOWN .... PAR ..... 1941 ..... WILLIAM BOYD
___WESTWARD HO .... REP ..... 1942 ..... TYLER/STEELE
___RAIDERS OF THE SOUTH .... MON .... 1947 ..... JOHNNY MACK BROWN
___ROBIN HOOD OF MONTERREY ..... MON .... 1947 ..... GILBERT ROLAND

LINDA BRENT

___RED RIVER VALLEY .... REP ..... 1941 ..... ROY ROGERS
___BELOW THE BORDER .... MON .... 1942 ..... JONES/McCOY
___DEATH VALLEY RANGERS .... MON .... 1943 ..... THE TRAIL BLAZERS
___LARAMIE TRAIL .... REP ..... 1944 ..... BOB LIVINGSTON

MARY BRIAN

___THE LIGHT OF THE WESTERN ...... PAR ..... 1930 ..... RICHARD ARLEN
STARS
___GUN SMOKE .... PAR ..... 1931 ..... RICHARD ARLEN
___CALABOOSE .... UA .... 1943 ..... JIMMY ROGERS

LOIS BRIDGE

___SINGLE HANDED SAUNDERS .... MON .... 1932 ..... TOM TYLER
___WYOMING WHIRLWIND .... KEN ..... 1932 ..... LANE CHANDLER
___RODEO RHYTHM .... PRC ..... 1942 ..... FRED SCOTT

___RIDERS IN THE SKY ....COL .....1949.....GENE AUTRY
___RIDERS OF WHISTLING PINE ....COL .....1949.....GENE AUTRY

VIRGINIA BRISSAC

___WAGONS WESTWARD ....REP .....1940.....CHESTER MORRIS
___THE DALTONS RIDE AGAIN ....UNI ......1945.....ALAN CURTIS
___IN OLD LOS ANGELES ....REP .....1948.....BILL ELLIOTT
___THE LAST BANDIT ....REP .....1949.....BILL ELLIOTT

BARBARA BRITTON

___SECRETS OF THE WASTELAND ...PAR .....1941.....WILLIAM BOYD
___ALBUQUERQUE ....PAR .....1948.....RANDOLPH SCOTT
___LOADED PISTOLS ....COL .....1949.....GENE AUTRY
___BANDIT QUEEN ....LIP ....1950.....BARBARA BRITTON

DORIS BROOK

___THE LONE BANDIT ....EMP .....1934.....LANE CHANDLER
___WILDERNESS MAIL ....AMB .....1935.....KERMIT MAYNARD
___DEFYING THE LAW ....AME .....1935.....TED WELLS
___BORDER GUNS ....AYW ....1935.....BILL CODY
___THE PHANTOM COWBOY ....AYW ....1935.....TED WELLS

LUCILLE BROWN

___LAST OF THE DUANES ....FOX .....1930.....GEORGE O'BRIEN
___THE TEXAN ....PRN .....1932.....BUFFALO BILL, JR.
___KING OF THE ARENA ....UNI ......1933.....KEN MAYNARD
___BRAND OF HATE ....SUP .....1934.....BOB STEELE
___TEXAS TERROR...............................MON ....1935.....JOHN WAYNE
___RAINBOW VALLEY ....MON ....1935.....JOHN WAYNE
___WESTERN FRONTIER ....COL .....1935.....KEN MAYNARD
___TUMBLING TUMBLEWEEDS ....REP .....1935.....GENE AUTRY
___THE CROOKED TRAIL ....SUP .....1936.....JOHNNY MACK BROWN
___CHEYENNE RIDES AGAIN ....VIC ....1937.....TOM TYLER

RENO BROWNE

___UNDER ARIZONA SKIES ....MON ....1946.....JOHNNY MACK BROWN
___GENTLEMEN FROM TEXAS ....MON ....1946.....JOHNNY MACK BROWN
___RAIDERS OF THE SOUTH ....MON ....1947.....JOHNNY MACK BROWN
___THE LAW COMES TO GUNSIGHT .MON ....1947.....JOHNNY MACK BROWN
___FRONTIER AGENT ....MON ....1948.....JOHNNY MACK BROWN
___SHADOWS OF THE WEST ....MON ....1949.....WHIP WILSON
___ACROSS THE RIO GRANDE ....MON ....1949.....JIMMY WAKELY
___WEST OF ELDORADO ....MON ....1949.....JOHNNY MACK BROWN
___HAUNTED TRAILS ....MON ....1949.....WHIP WILSON
___RIDERS OF THE DUSK ....MON ....1949.....WHIP WILSON

___RANGE LAND ....MON ....1949.....WHIP WILSON
___FENCE RIDERS ....MON ....1950.....WHIP WILSON
___GUNSLINGERS.......................................MON ....1950.....WHIP WILSON

Reno Browne with Riley Hill, Andy Clyde, and Whip Wilson

JAN BRYANT

___SHADOWS ON THE RANGE ....MON ....1946.....JOHNNY MACK BROWN
___SILVER RANGE ....MON ....1946.....JOHNNY MACK BROWN
___FLASHING GUNS ....MON ....1947.....JOHNNY MACK BROWN
___COWBOY CAVALIER ....MON ....1948.....JIMMY WAKELY
___CRASHING THRU.................................MON ....1949.....WHIP WILSON

JOYCE BRYANT

___TRIGGER SMITH ....MON ....1939.....JACK RANDALL
___ACROSS THE PLAINS ....MON ....1939.....JACK RANDALL
___FIGHTING RENEGADE ....VIC.......1939.....TIM McCOY
___TRIGGER FINGERS ....VIC.......1939.....TIM McCOY
___THE SAGEBRUSH FAMILY ....PRC .....1940.....BOBBY CLARK
TRAILS WEST

DOROTHY BURGESS

___LASCA OF THE RIO GRANDE ....UNI.......1931.....LEO CARRILLO

___RUSTY RIDES ALONE ....COL .....1933.....TIM McCOY
___LONE STAR RANGER......................20T ......1942.....JOHN KIMBROUGH

KATHLEEN BURKE

___SUNSET PASS.................................PAR .....1933.....RANDOLPH SCOTT
___ROCKY MOUNTAIN MYSTERY.......PAR .....1935.....RANDOLPH SCOTT
___NEVADA ....PAR .....1935.....BUSTER CRABBE

MARION BURNS

___OKLAHOMA JIM ....MON ....1931.....BILL CODY
___THE GOLDEN WEST.........................FOX .....1932.....GEORGE O'BRIEN
___THE DAWN RIDER ....MON ....1935.....JOHN WAYNE
___PARADISE CANYON.........................MON ....1935.....JOHN WAYNE

SUSAN CABOT

___THE DUEL AT SILVER CREEK ....UNI ......1952.....AUDIE MURPHY
___GUNSMOKE ....UNI ......1953.....AUDIE MURPHY
___RIDE CLEAR OF DIABLO ....UNI ......1953.....AUDIE MURPHY

CECILIA CALLEJO

___OUTLAW EXPRESS ....UNI ......1938.....BOB BAKER
___THE RENEGADE RANGER ....RKO .....1938.....GEORGE O'BRIEN
___THE CISCO KID RETURNS ....MON ....1945.....DUNCAN RENALDO

ANNA CAMARGO (ANITA)

___LAWLESS LAND ....REP .....1937.....JOHNNY MACK BROWN
___DESPERATE TRAILS ....UNI ......1939.....JOHNNY MACK BROWN
___GUN TO GUN ....WB ....1944.....ROBERT SHAYNE
___TWILIGHT ON THE RIO GRANDE ..REP .....1947.....GENE AUTRY

NINA CAMPANA

___SUNSET OF POWER ....UNI ......1936.....BUCK JONES
___IT HAPPENED OUT WEST ....FOX .....1937.....PAUL KELLY
___ROOTIN' TOOTIN' RHYTHM ....REP .....1937.....GENE AUTRY
___OUTLAW EXPRESS ....UNI ......1938.....BOB BAKER
___ARIZONA ....COL .....1940.....WILLIAM HOLDEN
___TWILIGHT ON THE RIO GRANDE ..REP .....1947.....GENE AUTRY

KATE CAMPBELL

___GHOST CITY....................................MON ....1932.....BILL CODY
___GHOST VALLEY ....RKO .....1932.....TOM KEENE
___COME ON TARZAN ....WW ......1932.....KEN MAYNARD

PEGGY CAMPBELL

___WHEN A MAN SEES RED ....UNI ......1934.....BUCK JONES

___STONE OF SILVER CREEK ....UNI.......1935.....BUCK JONES
___BIG CALIBRE ....SUP .....1935.....BOB STEELE

RITA CANSINO (SEE RITA HAYWORTH)

CLAIRE CARLETON

___GREAT TRAIN ROBBERY ....REP .....1941.....BOB STEELE
___GUN TOWN ....UNI.......1945.....KIRBY GRANT
___THAT TEXAS JAMBOREE ....COL .....1946.....KEN CURTIS
___BAD MEN OF TOMBSTONE ....AA ....1949.....BARRY SULLIVAN
___SATAN'S CRADLE ....UA ....1949.....DUNCAN RENALDO

JEAN CARLIN

___SIX GUN MAN ....PRC .....1946.....BOB STEELE
___CARAVAN TRAIL ....PRC .....1946.....EDDIE DEAN
___GHOST OF HIDDEN VALLEY..........PRC .....1946.....BUSTER CRABBE
___SONG OF THE SIERRAS.................MON ....1946.....JIMMY WAKELY
___WILD WEST ....PRC .....1946.....EDDIE DEAN

JEAN CARMEN

___BORN TO BATTLE ....REL......1935.....TOM TYLER
___GUNSMOKE RANCH........................REP .....1937.....LIVINGSTON/CORRIGAN
___ARIZONA GUNFIGHTER ....REP .....1937.....BOB STEELE
___IN OLD MONTANA ....SPE .....1939.....FRED SCOTT
___CRASHING THRU............................MON ....1939.....JIM NEWILL
___SMOKEY TRAILS.............................MET .....1939.....BOB STEELE

VIRGINIA CARPENTER

___ROLLING HOME TO TEXAS............MON ....1940.....TEX RITTER
___OUTLAWS OF THE RIO GRANDE..PRC .....1941.....TIM McCOY
___THE LONE STAR VIGILANTES.......COL .....1942.....ELLIOTT/RITTER
___GHOST TOWN LAW ....MON ....1942.....JONES/McCOY

MARY CARR

___THE UTAH KID.................................TIF ....1930.....REX LEASE
___THE FIGHTING MARSHAL ....COL .....1931.....TIM McCOY
___THE FIGHTING FOOL ....COL .....1932.....TIM McCOY
___FORBIDDEN TRAIL ....COL .....1932.....BUCK JONES
___GUN LAW ....MAJ......1933.....JACK HOXIE
___WEST OF RAINBOW'S END............MON ....1938.....TIM McCOY
___OREGON TRAIL ....REP .....1945.....SUNSET CARSON

ALMA CARROLL

___PARDON MY GUN ....COL .....1942.....CHARLES STARRETT
___A TORNADO IN THE SADDLE ....COL .....1942.....RUSSELL HAYDEN

___SILVER CITY RAIDERS ....COL .....1943.....RUSSELL HAYDEN
___WYOMING HURRICANE ....COL .....1944.....RUSSELL HAYDEN

VIRGINIA CARROLL

___A TENDERFOOT GOES WEST ....HOF .....1936.....RUSSELL GLEASON
___OKLAHOMA TERROR ....MON ....1939.....JACK RANDALL
___THE MASKED RIDER.......................UNI ......1941.....JOHNNY MACK BROWN
___THE PHANTOM COWBOY..............REP .....1941.....DON BARRY
___RAIDERS OF THE WEST ....PRC .....1942.....BOYD/DAVIS/POWELL
___PRAIRIE GUNSMOKE ....COL .....1942.....ELLIOTT/RITTER
___THE LAST ROUNDUP ....COL .....1947.....GENE AUTRY
___FRONTIER AGENT...........................MON ....1948.....JOHNNY MACK BROWN
___OVERLAND TRAILS ....MON ....1948.....JOHNNY MACK BROWN
___TRIGGERMAN ....MON ....1948.....JOHNNY MACK BROWN
___BAD MEN OF TOMBSTONE ....AA ....1949.....BARRY SULLIVAN
___CRASHIN' THRU ....MON ....1949.....WHIP WILSON
___RIDERS OF THE WHISTLING PINESCOL .....1949.....GENE AUTRY
___THE BLAZING SUN ....COL .....1950.....GENE AUTRY

LYNN CARVER

___MAN FROM CHEYENNE..................REP .....1942.....ROY ROGERS
___SUNSET ON THE DESERT ....REP .....1942.....ROY ROGERS
___LAW OF THE VALLEY......................MON ....1945.....JOHNNY MACK BROWN
___FLAME OF THE WEST.....................MON ....1945.....JOHNNY MACK BROWN
___DRIFTING ALONG ....MON ....1946.....JOHNNY MACK BROWN
___CROSSED TRAILS ....MON ....1948.....JOHNNY MACK BROWN

MARY CASTLE

___PRAIRIE ROUNDUP ....COL .....1951.....CHARLES STARRETT
___TEXANS NEVER CRY ....COL .....1951.....GENE AUTRY
___GUNSMOKE ....UNI ......1953.....AUDIE MURPHY

PEGGIE CASTLE

___WAGONS WEST ....UNI ......1952.....ROD CAMERON
___GUNSMOKE ....UNI ......1954.....JOCK MAHONEY
___RIDE CLEAR OF DIABLO ....UNI ......1954.....AUDIE MURPHY
___JESSIE JAMES' WOMEN ....UA ....1954.....DON BARRY
___OVERLAND PACIFIC ....UA ....1954.....JOCK MAHONEY

JANET CHANDLER

___THE GOLDEN WEST.........................FOX .....1932.....GEORGE O'BRIEN
___COWBOY HOLIDAY ....BEA .....1935.....GUINN WILLIAMS
___CYCLONE OF THE SADDLE ....SUP .....1935.....REX LEASE
___ROUGH RIDING RANGER...............S&S .....1935.....REX LEASE

ALMA CHESTER

___THE SUNDOWN TRAIL .... RKO ..... 1931 ..... TOM KEENE
___WHEN A MAN RIDES ALONE .... FM........ 1933 ..... TOM TYLER
___THE DUDE RANGER .... FOX ..... 1934 ..... GEORGE O'BRIEN
___COWBOY HOLIDAY .... BEA ..... 1935 ..... GUINN WILLIAMS
___THE OLD WYOMING TRAIL .... COL ..... 1937 ..... CHARLES STARRETT

DOROTHY CHRISTIE (CHRISTY)

___ROUGH RIDERS ROUNDUP .... REP ..... 1939 ..... ROY ROGERS
___SIERRA SUE .... REP ..... 1941 ..... GENE AUTRY
___THE COWBOY AND THE SENORITAREP ..... 1944 ..... ROY ROGERS

VIRGINIA CHRISTINE

___RAIDERS OF GHOST CITY (SERIAL) UNI .... 1944 ..... DENNIS MOORE
___THE OLD TEXAS TRAIL .... UNI .... 1944 ..... ROD CAMERON
___PHANTOM OF THE PLAINS .... REP ..... 1945 ..... BILL ELLIOTT

JAN CLAYTON (JANE)

___IN OLD MEXICO .... PAR ..... 1938 ..... WILLIAM BOYD
___THE LLANO KID .... PAR ..... 1939 ..... TITO GUIZAR
___SUNSET TRAIL .... PAR ..... 1939 ..... WILLIAM BOYD
___THE SHOWDOWN .... PAR ..... 1940 ..... WILLIAM BOYD
___SIX GUN GOLD .... RKO ..... 1941 ..... TIM HOLT
___THE WOLF HUNTERS .... MON .... 1949 ..... KIRBY GRANT

IRIS CLIVE

___RENEGADES OF THE RIO GRANDE UNI .... 1945 ..... ROD CAMERON
___THE LONESOME TRAIL .... MON .... 1945 ..... JIMMY WAKELY
___WEST OF THE ALAMO .... MON .... 1946 ..... JIMMY WAKELY
___SONG OF THE SIERRAS .... MON .... 1946 ..... JIMMY WAKELY

PHYLLIS COATES

___OUTLAWS OF TEXAS .... MON .... 1950 ..... WHIP WILSON
___MAN FROM SONORA .... MON .... 1951 ..... JOHNNY MACK BROWN
CANYON RAIDERS .... MON .... 1951 ..... WHIP WILSON
___NEVADA BADMEN .... MON .... 1951 ..... WHIP WILSON
___OKLAHOMA JUSTICE .... MON .... 1951 ..... JOHNNY MACK BROWN
___THE LONGHORN .... MON .... 1951 ..... BILL ELLIOTT
___STAGE TO BLUE RIVER .... MON .... 1951 ..... WHIP WILSON
___THE GUNMAN .... MON .... 1952 ..... WHIP WILSON
___FARGO .... MON .... 1952 ..... BILL ELLIOTT
___CANYON AMBUSH .... MON .... 1952 ..... JOHNNY MACK BROWN
___WYOMING ROUNDUP .... MON .... 1952 ..... WHIP WILSON
___THE MAVERICK .... MON .... 1952 ..... BILL ELLIOTT

___SCORCHING FURY .... FRA ..... 1952 ..... RICHARD DEVON
___MARSHAL OF CEDAR ROCK .... REP ..... 1953 ..... ALLAN LANE
___TOPEKA .... MON .... 1953 ..... BILL ELLIOTT
___EL PASO STAMPEDE .... REP ..... 1953 ..... ALLAN LANE

Phylllis Coates with Jim Bannon

MABEL COLCORD

___SMOKE TREE RANGE .... UNI ...... 1937 ..... BUCK JONES
___SUDDEN BILL DORN .... UNI ...... 1937 ..... BUCK JONES
___THE MYSTERIOUS RIDER .... PAR ..... 1938 ..... DOUGLAS DUMBRILLE

CLAUDIA COLEMAN

___SON OF THE BORDER .... RKO ..... 1933 ..... TOM KEENE
___THE COUNTRY BEYOND .... FOX ..... 1936 ..... PAUL KELLY
___RUSTLER'S VALLEY .... PAR ..... 1937 ..... WILLIAM BOYD

MILDRED COLES

___SONG OF THE DRIFTER .... MON .... 1948 ..... JIMMY WAKELY
___OKLAHOMA BADLANDS .... REP ..... 1948 ..... ALLAN LANE
___BACK TRAIL .... MON .... 1948 ..... JOHNNY MACK BROWN
___MARSHAL OF AMARILLO .... REP ..... 1948 ..... ALLAN LANE
___DESPERADOES OF DODGE CITY . REP ..... 1948 ..... ALLAN LANE

LOIS COLLIER

___OUTLAWS OF THE CHEROKEE ..... REP ..... 1941 ..... TYLER/STEELE
TRAIL
___GAUCHOS OF EL DORADO .... REP ..... 1941 ..... TYLER/STEELE
___WEST OF CIMARRON .... REP ..... 1941 ..... TYLER/STEELE
___RAIDERS OF THE RANGE .... REP ..... 1942 ..... TYLER/STEELE
___WESTWARD HO .... REP ..... 1942 ..... TYLER/STEELE
___THE PHANTOM PLAINSMAN .... REP ..... 1942 ..... TYLER/STEELE

___SANTA FE SCOUTS .... REP ..... 1943 ..... TYLER/STEELE
___WILD BEAUTY .... UNI .... 1946 ..... DON PORTER

BETTY COMPSON

___GOD'S COUNTRY AND THE MAN .. MON .... 1937 ..... TOM KEENE
___TWO GUN JUSTICE .... MON .... 1938 ..... RUSSELL HAYDEN
___COWBOYS FROM TEXAS .... REP ..... 1939 ..... LIVINGSTON/RENALDO

JOYCE COMPTON

___FIGHTING FOR JUSTICE .... COL ..... 1932 ..... TIM McCOY
___VALLEY OF THE LAWLESS .... SUP ..... 1936 ..... JOHNNY MACK BROWN
___SILVER SPURS .... REP ..... 1943 ..... ROY ROGERS

LITA CONWAY

___TRAILING DOUBLE TROUBLE .... MON .... 1940 ..... CORRIGAN/KING
___SADDLE MOUNTAIN ROUNDUP .... REP ..... 1942 ..... ALLAN LANE
___YUKON PATROL .... REP ..... 1942 ..... ALLAN LANE

INEZ COOPER

___NORTH OF THE BORDER .... SG .... 1946 ..... RUSSELL HAYDEN
___'NEATH CANADIAN SKIES .... SG .... 1946 ..... RUSSELL HAYDEN
___RIDING THE CALIFORNIA TRAIL ... MON .... 1947 ..... GILBERT ROLAND
___BORDER TREASURE .... RKO ..... 1950 ..... TIM HOLT

LITA CORTEZ

___THREE ON THE TRAIL .... PAR ..... 1936 ..... WILLIAM BOYD
___REBELLION .... RKO ..... 1936 ..... TOM KEENE
___ARIZONA GANGBUSTERS .... PRC ..... 1940 ..... TIM McCOY

CATHERINE COTTER

___THE TEXAS RAMBLER .... SPE ..... 1935 ..... BILL CODY
___OUTLAWS OF THE RANGE .... SPE ..... 1935 ..... BILL CODY
___PINTO RUSTLERS .... REL ...... 1936 ..... TOM TYLER
___SUNDOWN SAUNDERS .... SUP ..... 1936 ..... BOB STEELE

CAROLINA COTTON

___OUTLAWS OF THE ROCKIES .... COL ..... 1945 ..... CHARLES STARRETT
___SONG OF THE PRAIRIE .... COL ..... 1945 ..... KEN CURTIS
___TEXAS PANHANDLE .... COL ..... 1945 ..... CHARLES STARRETT
___COWBOY BLUES .... COL ..... 1946 ..... KEN CURTIS
___SINGING ON THE TRAIL .... COL ..... 1946 ..... KEN CURTIS
___THAT TEXAS JAMBOREE .... COL ..... 1946 ..... KEN CURTIS
___SMOKEY RIVER SERENADE .... COL ..... 1947 ..... PAUL CAMPBELL
___SMOKEY MOUNTAIN MELODY ...... COL ..... 1948 ..... ROY ACUFF
___STALLION CANYON .... AST ...... 1949 ..... KEN CURTIS

___APACHE COUNTRY .... COL ..... 1952..... GENE AUTRY
___ROUGH TOUGH WEST .... COL ..... 1952..... CHARLES STARRETT
___BLUE CANADIAN ROCKIES .... COL ..... 1952..... GENE AUTRY

KARLA COWAN

___RIDERS OF RIO .... RP .... 1931 ..... LANE CHANDLER
___THE GALLOPING KID .... IMP ...... 1932..... AL LANE
___ARIZONA CYCLONE .... IMP ...... 1934..... WALLY WALES

KATHRYN CRAWFORD

___SENOR AMERICANO .... UNI ...... 1930..... KEN MAYNARD
___MOUNTAIN JUSTICE .... UNI ...... 1930..... KEN MAYNARD
___THE CONCENTRATING KID .... UNI ...... 1930..... HOOT GIBSON

LOUISE CURRIE

___BILLY THE KID OUTLAWED .... PRC ..... 1940..... BOB STEELE
___THE PINTO KID .... COL ..... 1941 ..... CHARLES STARRETT
___DUDE COWBOY .... RKO ..... 1941 ..... TIM HOLT
___STARDUST ON THE SAGE .... REP ..... 1942..... GENE AUTRY
___FORTY THIEVES .... UA .... 1944..... WILLIAM BOYD
___GUN TOWN .... UNI ...... 1946..... KIRBY GRANT
___WILD WEST .... PRC ..... 1946..... EDDIE DEAN

Louise Currie with Kenne Duncan and Bob Steele

CAROLYN CURTIS (CLARENE, CLARISSA)

___MESQUITE BUCKAROO .... MET ..... 1939..... BOB STEELE

___PALS OF THE SILVER SAGE..........MON ....1940.....TEX RITTER
___THE KID FROM SANTA FE..............MON ....1940.....JACK RANDALL

ALICE DAHL

___THE WHIRLWIND ....COL .....1933.....TIM McCOY
___DEADWOOD ....FM........1933.....TOM TYLER
___COYOTE TRAILS..............................REL......1935.....TOM TYLER
___TWISTED RAILS ....IMP ......1935.....JACK DONOVAN

GAIL DAVIS

___THE FAR FRONTIER........................REP .....1948.....ROY ROGERS
___DEATH VALLEY GUNFIGHTER ......REP .....1949.....ALLAN LANE

Gail Davis

___FRONTIER INVESTIGATOR .... REP ..... 1949 ..... ALLAN LANE
___LAW OF THE GOLDEN WEST .... REP ..... 1949 ..... MONTE HALE
___BRAND OF FEAR .... MON .... 1949 ..... JIMMY WAKELY
___SOUTH OF DEATH VALLEY .... COL ..... 1949 ..... CHARLES STARRETT
___SONS OF NEW MEXICO .... COL ..... 1950 ..... GENE AUTRY
___TRAIL OF THE RUSTLERS .... COL ..... 1950 ..... CHARLES STARRETT
___WEST OF WYOMING .... MON .... 1950 ..... JOHNNY MACK BROWN
___SIX GUN MESA .... MON .... 1950 ..... JOHNNY MACK BROWN
___COW TOWN .... COL ..... 1950 ..... GENE AUTRY
___INDIAN TERRITORY .... COL ..... 1950 ..... GENE AUTRY
___TEXANS NEVER CRY .... COL ..... 1951 ..... GENE AUTRY
___WHIRLWIND .... COL ..... 1951 ..... GENE AUTRY
___SILVER CANYON .... COL ..... 1951 ..... GENE AUTRY
___YUKON MANHUNT .... MON .... 1951 ..... KIRBY GRANT
___VALLEY OF FIRE .... COL ..... 1951 ..... GENE AUTRY
___OVERLAND TELEGRAPH .... RKO ..... 1951 ..... TIM HOLT
___THE OLD WEST .... COL ..... 1952 ..... GENE AUTRY
___WAGON TEAM .... COL ..... 1952 ..... GENE AUTRY
___BLUE CANADIAN ROCKIES .... COL ..... 1952 ..... GENE AUTRY
___WINNING OF THE WEST .... COL ..... 1953 ..... GENE AUTRY
___ON TOP OF OLD SMOKY .... COL ..... 1953 ..... GENE AUTRY
___GOLDTOWN GHOST RAIDERS ...... COL ..... 1953 ..... GENE AUTRY
___PACK TRAIN .... COL ..... 1953 ..... GENE AUTRY

SUGAR DAWN

___PALS OF THE SILVER SAGE .... MON .... 1940 ..... TEX RITTER
___THE GOLDEN TRAIL .... MON .... 1940 ..... TEX RITTER
___WANDERERS OF THE WEST .... MON .... 1941 ..... TOM KEENE
___DYNAMITE CANYON .... MON .... 1941 ..... TOM KEENE
___RIDING THE SUNSET TRAIL .... MON .... 1941 ..... TOM KEENE
___LONE STAR LAW MEN .... MON .... 1941 ..... TOM KEENE
___ARIZONA ROUNDUP .... MON .... 1942 ..... TOM KEENE

LARAINE DAY

___THE LAW COMMANDS .... CRE ..... 1937 ..... TOM KEENE
___DOOMED AT SUNDOWN .... REP ..... 1937 ..... BOB STEELE
___BORDER G-MAN .... RKO ..... 1938 ..... GEORGE O'BRIEN
___PAINTED DESERT .... RKO ..... 1938 ..... GEORGE O'BRIEN
___ARIZONA LEGION .... RKO ..... 1939 ..... GEORGE O'BRIEN

MARCELINE DAY

___THE POCATELLO KID .... TIF .... 1931 ..... KEN MAYNARD
___THE FIGHTING FOOL .... COL ..... 1932 ..... TIM McCOY
___ARM OF THE LAW .... MON .... 1932 ..... REX BELL
___FROM BROADWAY TO CHEYENNE MON .... 1932 ..... REX BELL

Laraine Day with George O'Brien

Marceline Day, right, with Doris Hill and Jack Hoxie

___VIA PONY EXPRESS ....MAJ ..... 1933 ..... JACK HOXIE
___THE TELEGRAPH TRAIL ....WB .... 1933 ..... JOHN WAYNE
___THE FIGHTING PARSON ....ALL ...... 1933 ..... HOOT GIBSON

MARGIA DEAN

___RIM FIRE ....SG .... 1949 ..... JAMES MILLICAN
___GRAND CANYON ....SG .... 1949 ..... RICHARD ARLEN
___RED DESERT ....LIP .... 1950 ..... BARBARA BRITTON
___WESTERN PACIFIC AGENT ....LIP .... 1951 ..... KENT TAYLOR

CLAUDIA DELL

___DESTRY RIDES AGAIN ....UNI ...... 1932 ..... TOM MIX

Claudia Dell with Tom Mix

___THE TRAIL'S END ....BEA .....1935.....CONWAY TEARLE
___GHOST PATROL ....PUR .....1936.....TIM McCOY
___BOOTS OF DESTINY ....GN ....1937.....KEN MAYNARD

MYRNA DELL

___RAIDERS OF RED GAP ....PRC .....1943.....BOB LIVINGSTON
___ARIZONA WHIRLWIND ....MON ....1944.....MAYNARD/STEELE
___GUNS OF HATE...............................RKO .....1948.....TIM HOLT

JEAN DEL VAL

___DRUMS OF THE DESERT ....MON ....1940.....RALPH BYRD
___TRIPLE JUSTICE ....RKO .....1940.....GEORGE O'BRIEN
___OUTLAWS OF THE DESERT ....PAR .....1941.....WILLIAM BOYD

ANNA DEMETRIO (ANN DIMETRIO)

___ARIZONA MAHONEY ....PAR .....1936.....JOE COOK
___IN OLD MEXICO ....PAR .....1938.....WILLIAM BOYD
___THE TEXANS ....PAR .....1938.....RANDOLPH SCOTT
___LAW OF THE PAMPAS ....PAR .....1939.....WILLIAM BOYD
___THE LLANO KID.................................PAR .....1939.....TITO GUIZAR
___YOUNG BUFFALO BILL ....REP .....1940.....ROY ROGERS
___THE BANDIT QUEEN ....LIP ....1950.....BARBARA BRITTON

NANCY DESHON

___SILENT VALLEY ....REL......1935.....TOM TYLER
___TOMBSTONE TERROR ....SUP .....1935.....BOB STEELE
___TRAIL OF TERROR ....SUP .....1935.....BOB STEELE
___WOLF RIDERS..................................REL......1935.....JACK PERRIN

DOROTHY DIX

___NEVADA BUCKAROO ....TIF ....1931.....BOB STEELE
___DRUM TAPS.......................................WW ......1933.....KEN MAYNARD
___WHEELS OF DESTINY ....UNI.......1934.....KEN MAYNARD
___SUNSET POWER ....UNI.......1936.....BUCK JONES
___GUNS AND GUITARS ....REP .....1936.....GENE AUTRY

JOAN DIXON

___THE LAW OF THE BADLANDS ....RKO .....1951.....TIM HOLT
___GUNPLAY..RKO .....1951.....TIM HOLT
___PISTOL HARVEST............................RKO .....1951.....TIM HOLT
___HOT LEAD ....RKO .....1951.....TIM HOLT
___DESERT PASSAGE..........................RKO .....1952.....TIM HOLT

JEFF DONNELL

___COWBOY CANTEEN ....COL .....1944.....CHARLES STARRETT

___SONG OF THE PRAIRIE ....COL .....1945.....KEN CURTIS
___COWBOY BLUES ....COL .....1946.....KEN CURTIS
___SINGING ON THE TRAIL ....COL .....1946.....KEN CURTIS
___THAT TEXAS JAMBOREE ....COL .....1946.....KEN CURTIS
___THROW A SADDLE ON A STAR .....COL .....1946.....KEN CURTIS
___MY PAL, RINGEYE ....COL .....1947.....DEAN/BURNETTE
___THE STAGECOACH KID ....RKO .....1949.....TIM HOLT
___OUTCASTS OF THE TRAIL ....REP .....1949.....MONTE HALE
___REDWOOD FOREST TRAIL ....REP .....1950.....REX ALLEN
___MASSACRE CANYON ....COL .....1954.....PHIL CAREY

MARY DORAN

___RIDIN' FOR JUSTICE ....COL .....1932.....BUCK JONES
___SUNSET RANGE ....FD ....1935.....HOOT GIBSON
___BORDER PATROLMAN ....FOX .....1936.....GEORGE O'BRIEN

CATHY DOWNS

___PANHANDLE ....MON ....1948.....ROD CAMERON
___SHORT GRASS ....MON ....1950.....ROD CAMERON
___BANDITS OF THE WEST ....REP .....1953.....ALLAN LANE

MAXINE DOYLE

___RIO GRANDE ROMANCE ....VIC ....1936.....EDDIE NUGENT
___ROUNDUP TIME IN TEXAS ....REP .....1937.....GENE AUTRY
___COME ON COWBOYS ....REP .....1937.....LIVINGSTON/CORRIGAN
___OVERLAND MAIL ROBBERY ....REP .....1943.....BILL ELLIOTT
___RAIDERS OF SUNSET PASS ....REP .....1943.....EDDIE DEW
___SAN FERNANDO VALLEY ....REP .....1944.....ROY ROGERS

CLAUDIA DRAKE

___BORDER PATROL ....UA ....1943.....WILLIAM BOYD
___FALSE COLORS ....UA ....1943.....WILLIAM BOYD
___GENTLEMAN FROM TEXAS ....MON ....1946.....JOHNNY MACK BROWN
___LAWLESS BREED ....UNI ......1946.....KIRBY GRANT
___LONE STAR MOONLIGHT ....COL .....1946.....KEN CURTIS
___RENEGADE GIRL ....SG ....1946.....ALAN CURTIS
___INDIAN AGENT ....RKO .....1948.....TIM HOLT
___THE COWBOY AND THE INDIANS .COL .....1949.....GENE AUTRY
___NORTHERN PATROL......................MON ....1953.....KIRBY GRANT

NANCY DREXEL

___PARTNERS ....RKO .....1932.....TOM KEENE
___LAW OF THE WEST ....WW ......1932.....BOB STEELE
___MASON OF THE MOUNTED ....MON ....1932.....BILL CODY
___MAN FROM HELL'S EDGES ....WW ......1932.....BOB STEELE

___TEXAS BUDDIES ....WW ...... 1932 ..... BOB STEELE

ADA BELL DRIVER

___MARK OF THE SPUR ....B4 .... 1932 ..... BOB CUSTER
___THE COWBOY AND THE BANDIT .. SPR ..... 1935 ..... REX LEASE
___TWISTED RAILS ....IMP ...... 1935 ..... JACK DONOVAN

CLAIRE DUBREY

___SOUTH OF THE BORDER ....REP ..... 1939 ..... GENE AUTRY
___BELLS OF CAPISTRANO ....REP ..... 1942 ..... GENE AUTRY
___LIGHTS OF OLD SANTA FE ....REP ..... 1944 ..... ROY ROGERS
___THE BELLS OF SAN FERNANDO ... SG .... 1947 ..... DONALD WOODS

STEFFI DUNA

___PHANTOM RAIDERS ....MON .... 1938 ..... TIM McCOY
___THE GIRL AND THE GAMBLER ...... RKO ..... 1939 ..... LEO CARILLO
___LAW OF THE PAMPAS ....PAR ..... 1939 ..... WILLIAM BOYD

JULIE DUNCAN

___TEXAS TERRORS ....REP ..... 1940 ..... DON BARRY
___WYOMING WILDCAT ....REP ..... 1941 ..... DON BARRY
___FUGITIVE VALLEY ....MON .... 1941 ..... CORRIGAN/KING
___TEXAS MANHUNT ....PRC ..... 1942 ..... BOYD/DAVIS/POWELL
___TEXAS TROUBLE SHOOTERS ....MON .... 1942 ..... CORRIGAN/KING
___ALONG THE SUNDOWN TRAIL ...... PRC ..... 1942 ..... BOYD/DAVIS/POWELL
___OVERLAND STAGECOACH ....PRC ..... 1942 ..... BOB LIVINGSTON
___HAUNTED RANCH ....MON .... 1943 ..... DAVID SHARPE
___BULLETS AND SADDLES ....MON .... 1943 ..... MOORE/KING
___COWBOY IN THE CLOUDS ....COL ..... 1943 ..... CHARLES STARRETT

PAMELA DUNCAN

___WHISTLING HILLS ....MON .... 1951 ..... JOHNNY MACK BROWN
___LAWLESS COWBOYS ....MON .... 1952 ..... WHIP WILSON
___BRONC RIDER ....MON .... 1952 ..... WHIP WILSON
___TWO-GUN MARSHAL ....UA .... 1953 ..... GUY MADISON

MAUDE EBURNE

___ROBBERS' ROOST ....FOX ..... 1933 ..... GEORGE O'BRIEN
___HOLLYWOOD COWBOY ....RKO ..... 1937 ..... GEORGE O'BRIEN
___RIDERS OF THE BLACK HILLS ...... REP ..... 1938 ..... LIVINGSTON/CORRIGAN
___MOUNTAIN RHYTHM ....REP ..... 1939 ..... GENE AUTRY
___COLORADO ....REP ..... 1940 ..... ROY ROGERS
___THE BORDER LEGION ....REP ..... 1940 ..... ROY ROGERS
___MAN FROM OKLAHOMA ....REP ..... 1945 ..... ROY ROGERS
___THE PLUNDERERS ....REP ..... 1948 ..... ROD CAMERON

PENNY EDWARDS

___NORTH OF THE GREAT DIVIDE ....REP .....1950.....ROY ROGERS
___SUNSET IN THE WEST ....REP .....1950.....ROY ROGERS
___TRAIL OF ROBIN HOOD ....REP .....1951.....ROY ROGERS
___SPOILERS OF THE PLAINS ....REP .....1951.....ROY ROGERS
___HEART OF THE ROCKIES ....REP .....1951.....ROY ROGERS
___IN OLD AMARILLO ....REP .....1951.....ROY ROGERS
___UTAH WAGON TRAIN.......................REP .....1951.....REX ALLEN
___CAPTIVE OF BILLY THE KID ....REP .....1952.....ALLAN LANE

SARAH EDWARDS

___CALABOOSE......................................UA ....1943.....JIMMY ROGERS
___SONG OF ARIZONA..........................REP .....1946.....ROY ROGERS
___CALIFORNIA FIREBRAND...............REP .....1948.....MONTE HALE

SALLY EILERS

___LONG LONG TRAIL...........................UNI ......1929.....HOOT GIBSON
___ROARING RANCH ....UNI ......1930.....HOOT GIBSON
___TRIGGER TRICKS ....UNI ......1930.....HOOT GIBSON
___CLEARING THE RANGE..................ALL ......1931.....HOOT GIBSON
___A HOLY TERROR ....FOX .....1931.....GEORGE O'BRIEN
___CORONER CREEK...........................COL .....1948.....RANDOLPH SCOTT
___STAGE TO TUCSON ....COL .....1951.....ROD CAMERON

EDYTHE ELLIOTT

___THE MEDICO OF PAINTED SPRINGS COL .....1941.....CHARLES STARRETT
___BULLETS FOR BANDITS ....COL .....1942.....ELLIOTT/RITTER
___VALLEY OF HUNTED MEN ....REP .....1942.....TYLER/STEELE
___COWBOY CANTEEN ....COL .....1944.....CHARLES STARRETT
___SANTA FE UPRISING ....REP .....1946.....ALLAN LANE
___THE FABULOUS TEXAN...................REP .....1947.....BILL ELLIOTT
___HOMESTEADERS OF PARADISE ..REP .....1947.....ALLAN LANE
VALLEY

KATHLEEN ELLIOTT

___STARS OVER ARIZONA ....MON ....1937.....JACK RANDALL
___PAROLED TO DIE ....REP .....1938.....BOB STEELE
___WEST OF RAINBOW'S END............MON ....1938.....TIM McCOY

FERN EMMETT

___TERROR OF THE PLAINS ....REP .....1935.....TOM TYLER
___THE OREGON TRAIL........................REP .....1936.....JOHN WAYNE
___RIDERS OF THE WHISTLING SKULL .REP .....1937.....LIVINGSTON/CORRIGAN
___COME ON COWBOYS ....REP .....1937.....LIVINGSTON/CORRIGAN
___OVERLAND STAGE RAIDERS ....REP .....1938.....WAYNE/CORRIGAN

___DESPERATE TRAILS .... UNI .... 1939 ..... JOHNNY MACK BROWN
___TRIPLE JUSTICE .... RKO ..... 1940 ..... GEORGE O'BRIEN
___SIX GUN GOLD .... RKO ..... 1941 ..... TIM HOLT
___JESSE JAMES AT BAY .... REP ..... 1941 ..... ROY ROGERS
___SONS OF THE PIONEERS .... REP ..... 1942 ..... ROY ROGERS
___SUNDOWN KID .... REP ..... 1942 ..... DON BARRY

ESTELITA (RODRIGUEZ)

___ALONG THE NAVAJO TRAIL .... REP ..... 1945 ..... ROY ROGERS
___ON THE OLD SPANISH TRAIL .... REP ..... 1947 ..... ROY ROGERS
___THE GAY RANCHERO .... REP ..... 1948 ..... ROY ROGERS
___OLD LOS ANGELES .... REP ..... 1948 ..... BILL ELLIOTT
___SUSANNA PASS .... REP ..... 1949 ..... ROY ROGERS
___THE GOLDEN STALLION .... REP ..... 1949 ..... ROY ROGERS
___TWILIGHT IN THE SIERRAS .... REP ..... 1950 ..... ROY ROGERS
___SUNSET IN THE WEST .... REP ..... 1950 ..... ROY ROGERS
___IN OLD AMARILLO .... REP ..... 1951 ..... ROY ROGERS

Estelita (Rodriguez) with Rex Allan and Nestor Paiva

___PALS OF THE GOLDEN WEST .... REP ..... 1951 ..... ROY ROGERS
___SOUTH PACIFIC TRAIL .... REP ..... 1952 ..... REX ALLEN

ESTHER ESTRELLA

___THE LIGHT OF THE WESTERN STARS ...... PAR ..... 1940 ..... RUSSELL HAYDEN
___THREE MEN FROM TEXAS .... PAR ..... 1940 ..... WILLIAM BOYD
___DOWN MEXICO WAY .... REP ..... 1941 ..... GENE AUTRY
___PRAIRIE PIONEERS .... REP ..... 1941 ..... THREE MESQUITEER
___PRAIRIE PALS .... PRC ..... 1942 ..... BOYD/DAVIS/POWELL
___UNDERCOVER MAN .... UA .... 1942 ..... WILLIAM BOYD

DALE EVANS

___THE COWBOY AND THE SENORITA . REP ..... 1944 ..... ROY ROGERS
___YELLOW ROSE OF TEXAS .... REP ..... 1944 ..... ROY ROGERS

Dale Evans with Roy Rogers

___SONG OF NEVADA .... REP ..... 1944 ..... ROY ROGERS
___SAN FERNANDO VALLEY .... REP ..... 1944 ..... ROY ROGERS
___LIGHTS OF OLD SANTA FE .... REP ..... 1944 ..... ROY ROGERS
___UTAH .... REP ..... 1945 ..... ROY ROGERS
___BELLS OF ROSARITA .... REP ..... 1945 ..... ROY ROGERS
___THE MAN FROM OKLAHOMA .... REP ..... 1945 ..... ROY ROGERS
___SUNSET IN EL DORADO .... REP ..... 1945 ..... ROY ROGERS
___DON'T FENCE ME IN .... REP ..... 1945 ..... ROY ROGERS
___ALONG THE NAVAJO TRAIL .... REP ..... 1945 ..... ROY ROGERS
___SONG OF ARIZONA .... REP ..... 1946 ..... ROY ROGERS
___RAINBOW OVER TEXAS .... REP ..... 1946 ..... ROY ROGERS
___MY PAL TRIGGER .... REP ..... 1946 ..... ROY ROGERS
___UNDER NEVADA SKIES .... REP ..... 1946 ..... ROY ROGERS
___ROLL ON TEXAS MOON .... REP ..... 1946 ..... ROY ROGERS
___HOME IN OKLAHOMA .... REP ..... 1946 ..... ROY ROGERS
___OUT CALIFORNIA WAY .... REP ..... 1946 ..... MONTE HALE
___HELDORADO .... REP ..... 1947 ..... ROY ROGERS
___APACHE ROSE .... REP ..... 1947 ..... ROY ROGERS
___BELLS OF SAN ANGELO .... REP ..... 1947 ..... ROY ROGERS
___SUSANNA PASS .... REP ..... 1949 ..... ROY ROGERS
___DOWN DAKOTA WAY .... REP ..... 1949 ..... ROY ROGERS
___THE GOLDEN STALLION .... REP ..... 1949 ..... ROY ROGERS
___BELLS OF CORONADO .... REP ..... 1950 ..... ROY ROGERS
___TWILIGHT IN THE SIERRAS .... REP ..... 1950 ..... ROY ROGERS
___TRIGGER, JR. .... REP ..... 1950 ..... ROY ROGERS
___SOUTH OF CALIENTE .... REP ..... 1951 ..... ROY ROGERS
___PALS OF THE GOLDEN WEST .... REP ..... 1951 ..... ROY ROGERS

MURIEL EVANS

___THE THROWBACK .... UNI ..... 1935 ..... BUCK JONES
___THE NEW FRONTIER .... REP ..... 1935 ..... JOHN WAYNE
___SILVER SPURS .... UNI ..... 1936 ..... BUCK JONES
___CALL OF THE PRAIRIE .... PAR ..... 1936 ..... WILLIAM BOYD
___KING OF THE PECOS .... REP ..... 1936 ..... JOHN WAYNE
___THREE ON THE TRAIL .... PAR ..... 1936 ..... WILLIAM BOYD
___BOSS RIDER OF GUN CREEK .... UNI ..... 1936 ..... BUCK JONES
___SMOKE TREE RANGE .... UNI ..... 1937 ..... BUCK JONES
___RUSTLER'S VALLEY .... PAR ..... 1937 ..... WILLIAM BOYD
___LAW FOR TOMBSTONE .... UNI ..... 1937 ..... BUCK JONES
___BOSS OF LONELY VALLEY .... UNI ..... 1937 ..... BUCK JONES
___WESTBOUND STAGE .... MON ..... 1940 ..... TEX RITTER
___ROLL WAGONS, ROLL .... MON ..... 1940 ..... TEX RITTER

VIRGINIA BROWN FAIRE

___THE LONESOME TRAIL .... SYN ..... 1930 ..... CHARLES DELANEY

___TRAILS OF PERIL .... B4 .... 1930 ..... WALLY WALES
___BREED OF THE WEST .... B4 .... 1930 ..... WALLY WALES
___HELL'S VALLEY .... B4 .... 1931 ..... WALLY WALES
___ALIAS THE BAD MAN .... TIF .... 1931 ..... KEN MAYNARD
___TEX TAKES A HOLIDAY .... ARG ..... 1932 ..... WALLACE McDONALD
___THE LONE TRAIL .... SYN ..... 1932 ..... REX LEASE
___WEST OF THE DIVIDE .... MON .... 1934 ..... JOHN WAYNE
___RAINBOW RIDERS .... REL ...... 1934 ..... JACK PERRIN
___TRACY RIDES .... REL ...... 1935 ..... TOM TYLER

DOT FARLEY

___STRANGER FROM ARIZONA .... COL ..... 1938 ..... BUCK JONES
___LAWLESS VALLEY .... RKO ..... 1938 ..... GEORGE O'BRIEN
___SAN FERNANDO VALLEY .... REP ..... 1944 ..... ROY ROGERS

DOROTHY FAY

___FRONTIER SCOUT .... GN .... 1938 ..... GEORGE HOUSTON
___STRANGER FROM ARIZONA .... COL ..... 1938 ..... BUCK JONES
___LAW OF THE TEXAN .... COL ..... 1938 ..... BUCK JONES
___PRAIRIE JUSTICE .... UNI ...... 1938 ..... BOB BAKER
___SONG OF THE BUCKAROO .... MON .... 1939 ..... TEX RITTER
___TRIGGER PALS .... GN .... 1939 ..... JARRET/POWELL
___SUNDOWN ON THE PRAIRIE .... MON .... 1939 ..... TEX RITTER
___ROLLING WESTWARD .... MON .... 1939 ..... TEX RITTER
___RAINBOW OVER THE RANGE .... MON .... 1940 ..... TEX RITTER
___NORTH FROM THE LONE STAR .... COL ..... 1941 ..... BILL ELLIOTT

BLANCHE FEDERICI

___LAST OF THE DUANES .... FOX ..... 1930 ..... GEORGE O'BRIEN
___THE THUNDERING HERD .... PAR ..... 1933 ..... RANDOLPH SCOTT
___MAN OF THE FOREST .... PAR ..... 1933 ..... RANDOLPH SCOTT

EDITH FELLOWS

___RIDER OF DEATH VALLEY .... UNI ...... 1932 ..... TOM MIX
___LAW AND LAWLESS .... MAJ ..... 1932 ..... JACK HOXIE
___HEART OF THE RIO GRANDE .... REP ..... 1942 ..... GENE AUTRY
___STARDUST ON THE SAGE .... REP ..... 1942 ..... GENE AUTRY

CHARLOTTE FIELD

___HEART OF THE WEST .... PAR ..... 1936 ..... WILLIAM BOYD
___PRIDE OF THE WEST .... PAR ..... 1938 ..... WILLIAM BOYD
___THE MYSTERIOUS RIDER .... PAR ..... 1938 ..... DOUGLAS DUMBRILLE

MARY FIELD

___THE FIGHTING GRINGO .... RKO ..... 1939 ..... GEORGE O'BRIEN

___LEGION OF THE LAWLESS .... RKO ..... 1940 ..... GEORGE O'BRIEN
___THE TRAIL BLAZERS .... REP ..... 1940 ..... LIVINGSTON/STEELE

RUTH FINDLEY

___LAST OF THE CLINTONS .... AJAX .... 1935 ..... HARRY CAREY
___THE PECOS KID .... COM .... 1935 ..... FRED KOHLER, JR
___GHOST TOWN .... COM .... 1936 ..... HARRY CAREY
___HEROES OF THE ALAMO .... COL ..... 1937 ..... REX LEASE

EVELYN FINLEY

___ARIZONA FRONTIER .... MON .... 1940 ..... TEX RITTER
___DYNAMITE CANYON .... MON .... 1941 ..... TOM KEENE
___TRAIL RIDERS .... MON .... 1942 ..... SHARPE/KING
___COWBOY COMMANDOS .... MON .... 1943 ..... CORRIGAN/KING
___BLACK MARKET RUSTLER .... MON .... 1943 ..... CORRIGAN/KING
___VALLEY OF VENGEANCE .... PRC ..... 1944 ..... BUSTER CRABBE
___GHOST GUNS .... MON .... 1944 ..... JOHNNY MACK BROWN
___PRAIRIE RUSTLERS .... PRC ..... 1945 ..... BUSTER CRABBE
___SHERIFF OF MEDICINE BOW .... MON .... 1948 ..... JOHNNY MACK BROWN
___GUNNING FOR JUSTICE .... MON .... 1948 ..... JOHNNY MACK BROWN
___SUNDOWN RIDERS .... FE .... 1948 ..... JAY KIRBY

ALICE FLEMING

___OVERLAND MAIL ROBBERY .... REP ..... 1943 ..... BILL ELLIOTT
___TUSCON RAIDERS .... REP ..... 1944 ..... BILL ELLIOTT
___MARSHALL OF RENO .... REP ..... 1944 ..... BILL ELLIOTT
___SAN ANTONIO KID .... REP ..... 1944 ..... BILL ELLIOTT
___CHEYENNE WILDCAT .... REP ..... 1944 ..... BILL ELLIOTT
___VIGILANTES OF DODGE CITY .... REP ..... 1944 ..... BILL ELLIOTT
___SHERIFF OF LAS VEGAS .... REP ..... 1944 ..... BILL ELLIOTT
___GREAT STAGECOACH ROBBERY . REP ..... 1945 ..... BILL ELLIOTT
___LONE TEXAS RANGER .... REP ..... 1945 ..... BILL ELLIOTT
___PHANTOM OF THE PLAINS .... REP ..... 1945 ..... BILL ELLIOTT
___MARSHAL OF LAREDO .... REP ..... 1945 ..... BILL ELLIOTT
___COLORADO PIONEERS .... REP ..... 1945 ..... BILL ELLIOTT
___WAGON WHEELS WESTWARD ..... REP ..... 1945 ..... BILL ELLIOTT
___CALIFORNIA GOLD RUSH .... REP ..... 1946 ..... BILL ELLIOTT
___SUN VALLEY CYCLONE .... REP ..... 1946 ..... BILL ELLIOTT
___CONQUEST OF CHEYENNE .... REP ..... 1946 ..... BILL ELLIOTT
___SHERIFF OF REDWOOD VALLEY .. REP ..... 1946 ..... BILL ELLIOTT

CAROL FORMAN

___CODE OF THE WEST .... RKO ..... 1947 ..... JAMES WARREN
___GUNSMOKE .... AST ...... 1947 ..... NICK STUART
___THUNDER MOUNTAIN .... RKO ..... 1947 ..... TIM HOLT

___UNDER THE TONTO RIM ....RKO .....1947.....TIM HOLT
___BROTHERS IN THE SADDLE ....RKO .....1949.....TIM HOLT

KAY FORRESTER

___BLAZING GUNS ....MON ....1943.....MAYNARD/GIBSON
___SAN FERNANDO VALLEY ....REP .....1944.....ROY ROGERS
___SONG OF THE RANGE ....MON ....1944.....JIMMY WAKELY

HELEN FOSTER

___GHOST CITY.....................................MON ....1932.....BILL CODY
___SADDLE BUSTER.............................RKO .....1932.....TOM KEENE
___YOUNG BLOOD ....MON ....1932.....BOB STEELE
___THE BOILING POINT ....ALL ......1932.....HOOT GIBSON
___LUCKY LARRIGAN ....MON ....1932.....REX BELL

NOEL FRANCIS

___MY PAL, THE KING ....UNI ......1932.....TOM MIX
___STONE OF SILVER CREEK ....UNI ......1935.....BUCK JONES
___LEFT HANDED LAW.........................UNI ......1936.....BUCK JONES
___SUDDEN BILL DORN ....UNI ......1937.....BUCK JONES

JANE FRAZEE

___COWBOY CANTEEN ....COL .....1944.....CHARLES STARRETT
___THE BIG BONANZA..........................REP .....1944.....RICHARD ARLEN
___SWING IN THE SADDLE..................COL .....1944.....GUINN WILLIAMS
___SPRINGTIME IN THE SIERRAS......REP .....1947.....ROY ROGERS
___ON THE OLD SPANISH TRAIL........REP .....1947.....ROY ROGERS
___THE GAY RANCHERO ....REP .....1948.....ROY ROGERS
___UNDER CALIFORNIA STARS ....REP .....1948.....ROY ROGERS
___GRAND CANYON TRAIL..................REP .....1948.....ROY ROGERS
___LAST OF THE WILD HORSES ....LIP ....1948.....JIMMY ELLISON

BARBARA FRITCHIE

___THE LAST ROUNDUP ....PAR .....1934.....RANDOLPH SCOTT
___THUNDER MOUNTAIN......................20T ......1935.....GEORGE O'BRIEN
___WILD MUSTANG..............................AJA ......1935.....HARRY CAREY

KATHERINE FRYE (KAY, KATHY)

___ROARING LEAD ....REP .....1936.....LIVINGSTON/CORRIGAN
___MEXICALI ROSE ....REP .....1939.....GENE AUTRY
___HEART OF THE RIO GRANDE........REP .....1942.....GENE AUTRY
___CROSSED TRAILS ....MON ....1948.....JOHNNY MACK BROWN

BETTY FURNESS

___RENEGADES OF THE WEST ....RKO .....1932.....TOM KEENE

___SCARLET RIVER ....RKO ..... 1933 ..... TOM KEENE
___CROSSFIRE ....RKO ..... 1933 ..... TOM KEENE

JUNE GALE

___SWIFTY ....GN .... 1935 ..... HOOT GIBSON
___RAINBOW'S END ....FD .... 1935 ..... HOOT GIBSON
___THE RIDING AVENGER ....GN .... 1935 ..... HOOT GIBSON
___HEROES OF THE RANGE ....COL ..... 1936 ..... KEN MAYNARD

ROBERTA GALE

___MYSTERY RANCH ....REL ...... 1934 ..... TOM TYLER
___TERROR OF THE PLAINS ....REL ...... 1934 ..... TOM TYLER
___ALIAS JOHN LAW ....SUP ..... 1935 ..... BOB STEELE
___NO MANS' RANGE ....SUP ..... 1935 ..... BOB STEELE

Roberta Gale with Tom Tyler and Cast

BEVERLY GARLAND

___BITTER CREEK ....AA .... 1954 ..... BILL ELLIOTT
___THE DESPERADO ....AA .... 1954 ..... WAYNE MORRIS
___TWO GUNS AND A BADGE ....AA .... 1954 ..... WAYNE MORRIS

NANCY GATES

___COME ON DANGER ....RKO ..... 1942 ..... TIM HOLT
___NEVADA ....RKO ..... 1944 ..... ROBERT MITCHUM
___CHEYENNE TAKES OVER ....PRC ..... 1947 ..... LASH LARUE
___CHECK YOUR GUNS ....EL .... 1948 ..... EDDIE DEAN

___ROLL THUNDER ROLL .... EL .... 1949 ..... JIM BANNON
___RAWHIDE TRAIL .... AA .... 1950 ..... REX REASON

NANCY GAY

___THE MAN FROM THE RIO GRANDE REP ..... 1943 ..... DON BARRY
___OVERLAND MAIL ROBBERY .... REP ..... 1943 ..... BILL ELLIOTT
___PRIDE OF THE PLAINS .... REP ..... 1944 ..... BOB LIVINGSTON

GWEN GAZE

___PARTNERS OF THE PLAINS .... PAR ..... 1938 ..... WILLIAM BOYD
___BAR 20 JUSTICE .... PAR ..... 1938 ..... WILLIAM BOYD
___WEST OF PINTO BASIN .... MON .... 1940 ..... CORRIGAN/KING
___WRANGLERS' ROOST .... MON .... 1941 ..... CORRIGAN/KING
___UNDERGROUND RUSTLERS .... MON .... 1941 ..... CORRIGAN/KING
___TWO FISTED JUSTICE .... MON .... 1943 ..... CORRIGAN/KING

CARMELITA GERAGHTY

___MEN WITHOUT LAW .... COL ..... 1930 ..... BUCK JONES
___ROGUE OF THE RIO GRANDE .... WW ...... 1930 ..... JOSE BOHR
___THE TEXAS RANGER .... COL ..... 1931 ..... BUCK JONES
___FIGHTING THROUGH .... TIF .... 1934 ..... KEN MAYNARD

INA GEST (GUEST)

___THE GOLDEN TRAIL .... MON .... 1940 ..... TEX RITTER
___GUN CODE .... PRC ..... 1940 ..... TIM McCOY
___SIX GUN GOSPEL .... MON .... 1943 ..... JOHNNY MACK BROWN

HELEN GIBSON

___LAW AND LAWLESS .... MAJ ..... 1932 ..... JACK HOXIE
___KING OF THE ARENA .... UNI ...... 1933 ..... KEN MAYNARD
___WAY OF THE WEST .... SUP ..... 1934 ..... WALLY WALES
___WHEELS OF DESTINY .... UNI ...... 1934 ..... KEN MAYNARD
___CYCLONE OF THE SADDLE .... SUP ..... 1935 ..... REX LEASE
___CROOKED RIVER .... LIP .... 1950 ..... ELLISON/HAYDEN
___FAST ON THE DRAW .... LIP .... 1950 ..... ELLISON/HAYDEN

FRANCES GIFFORD

___BORDER VIGILANTES .... PAR ..... 1941 ..... WILLIAM BOYD
___AMERICAN EXPRESS .... UA .... 1942 ..... RICHARD DIX
___TOMBSTONE .... PAR ..... 1942 ..... RICHARD DIX

LILLIAN GILMORE

___RAWHIDE MAIL .... REL ...... 1934 ..... JACK PERRIN
___UNCONQUERED BANDIT .... REL ...... 1935 ..... TOM TYLER
___WOLF RIDERS .... REL ...... 1935 ..... JACK PERRIN

FRANCES GLADWIN

___WEST OF TEXAS ....PRC .....1943.....NEWILL/O'BRIEN
___WOLVES OF THE RANGE ....PRC .....1943.....BOB LIVINGSTON
___CATTLE STAMPEDE ....PRC .....1943.....BUSTER CRABBE
___FRONTIER OUTLAWS ....PRC .....1944.....BUSTER CRABBE
___THUNDERING GUNSLINGERS.......PRC .....1944.....BUSTER CRABBE
___STAGECOACH OUTLAWS ....PRC .....1945.....BUSTER CRABBE

MINNA GOMBELL

___THE RAINBOW TRAIL......................FOX .....1932.....GEORGE O'BRIEN
___DOOMED CARAVAN ....PAR .....1941.....WILLIAM BOYD
___WYOMING ....REP .....1947.....BILL ELLIOTT
___RETURN OF THE BADMEN ....RKO .....1948.....RANDOLPH SCOTT
___THE LAST BANDIT ....REP .....1949.....BILL ELLIOTT

MARY GORDON

___TEXAS CYCLONE ....COL .....1932.....TIM McCOY
___THE WHIRLWIND ....COL .....1933.....TIM McCOY
___THE MAN FROM HELL ....KEN .....1934.....REB RUSSELL
___ONE MAN JUSTICE..........................COL .....1937.....CHARLES STARRETT
___RACKETEERS OF THE RANGE .....RKO .....1939.....GEORGE O'BRIEN
___MARSHALL OF MESA CITY ....RKO .....1939.....GEORGE O'BRIEN
___DEPUTY MARSHAL.........................LIP ....1949.....JON HALL
___HAUNTED TRAILS ....MON ....1949.....WHIP WILSON
___WEST OF WYOMING ....MON ....1950.....JOHNNY MACK BROWN

DOROTHY GRANGER

___THE FIGHTING FOOL ....COL .....1932.....TIM McCOY
___BLUE MONTANA SKIES ....REP .....1939.....GENE AUTRY
___NORTH TO THE KLONDIKE ....UNI.......1942.....BRODERICK CRAWFORD
___SUNSET IN ELDORADO ....REP .....1945.....ROY ROGERS
___MARSHALL OF LAREDO ....REP .....1945.....BILL ELLI0TT
___UNDER WESTERN SKIES..............UNI.......1945.....NOAH BEERY JR..
___CACTUS CUTUP ....RKO .....1949.....LEON ERROL

FRANCES GRANT

___THUNDER MOUNTAIN.....................20T.......1935.....GEORGE O'BRIEN
___RED RIVER VALLEY ....REP .....1936.....GENE AUTRY
___OH SUSANNA ....REP .....1936.....GENE AUTRY
___THE TRAITOR..................................PUR .....1936.....TIM McCOY
___CAVALRY ....REP .....1936.....BOB STEELE

BEATRICE GRAY

___THE UTAH KID.................................MON ....1944.....GIBSON/STEELE
___TRIGGER LAW..................................MON ....1945.....JOHNNY MACK BROWN

___TRAIL TO VENGEANCE ....UNI ......1945.....KIRBY GRANT

SHIRLEY GREY

___ONE MAN LAW ....COL .....1932.....BUCK JONES
___TEXAS CYCLONE ....COL .....1932.....TIM McCOY
___THE RIDING TORNADO ....COL .....1932.....TIM McCOY
___CORNERED ....COL .....1932.....TIM McCOY
___TREASON ....COL .....1933.....BUCK JONES
___BEYOND THE LAW ....COL .....1934.....TIM McCOY

VIRGINIA GREY

___SECRET VALLEY ....20T ......1937.....RICHARD ARLEN
___BELLS OF CAPISTRANO ....REP .....1942.....GENE AUTRY
___IDAHO ....REP .....1943.....ROY ROGERS
___WYOMING ....REP .....1947.....BILL ELLIOTT

NINA GUILBERT

___CAVALCADE OF THE WEST...........DIV.......1936.....HOOT GIBSON
___TRIGGER PALS ....GN ....1939.....JARRETT/POWELL
___SAGEBRUSH FAMILY TRAILS........PRC .....1940.....BOBBY CLARK
___OUTLAWS OF THE DESERT ....PAR .....1941.....WILLIAM BOYD
___THREE DESPERATE MEN ....LIP ....1951.....PRESTON FOSTER
___DESERT PURSUIT ....MON ....1952.....WAYNE MORRIS
___THE FIGHTING LAWMAN ....AA ....1953.....WAYNE MORRIS
___THE FORTY NINERS ....AA ....1954.....BILL ELLIOTT

DOROTHY GULLIVER

___UNDER MONTANA SKIES...............TIF ....1930.....KENNETH HARLAN
___IN OLD CHEYENNE ....WW ......1931.....REX LEASE
___THE FIGHTING MARSHAL ....COL .....1931.....TIM McCOY
___OUTLAW JUSTICE ....MAJ .....1932.....JACK HOXIE
___THE PECOS DANDY ....SEC .....1934.....GEORGE J LEWIS
___FIGHTING CABALLERO ....SPR .....1935.....REX LEASE
___IN EARLY ARIZONA ....COL .....1938.....BILL ELLIOTT
___LONE STAR PIONEERS ....COL .....1939.....BILL ELLIOTT

ANN GWYNNE

___OKLAHOMA FRONTIER ....UNI ......1939.....JOHNNY MACK BROWN
___BAD MAN FROM RED BUTTE ....UNI ......1940.....JOHNNY MACK BROWN
___ROAD AGENT ....UNI ......1941.....DICK FORAN
___FRONTIER BADMAN........................UNI ......1943.....ROBERT PAIGE
___PANHANDLE ....MON ....1948.....ROD CAMERON
___CALL OF THE KLONDIKE................MON ....1950.....KIRBY GRANT
___THE BLAZING SUN ....COL .....1950.....GENE AUTRY
___KING OF THE BULLWHIP................WA ....1951.....LASH LARUE

PAULINE HADDEN

___THE COWBOY FROM SUNDOWN..MON ....1940.....TEX RITTER
___ARIZONA GANGBUSTERS..............PRC .....1940.....TIM McCOY
___RIDERS OF BLACK MOUNTAIN .....PRC .....1940.....TIM McCOY

ELLEN HALL

___OUTLAWS OF STAMPEDE PASS...MON ....1943.....JOHNNY MACK BROWN
___RAIDERS OF THE BORDER ....MON ....1944.....JOHNNY MACK BROWN
___LUMBERJACK...................................UA.........1944.....WILLIAM BOYD
___RANGE LAW ....MON ....1944.....JOHNNY MACK BROWN
___CALL OF THE ROCKIES..................REP .....1944.....SUNSET CARSON
___BRAND OF THE DEVIL ....PRC .....1944.....NEWILL/O'BRIEN
___THUNDER TOWN ....PRC .....1946.....BOB STEELE
___LAWLESS CODE ....MON ....1949.....JIMMY WAKELY

LOIS HALL

___ROARING WESTWARD ....MON ....1949.....JIMMY WAKELY
___HORSEMEN OF THE SIERRAS ......COL .....1949.....CHARLES STARRETT
___TEXAS DYNAMO ....COL .....1950.....CHARLES STARRETT
___FRONTIER OUTPOST.......................COL .....1950.....CHARLES STARRETT
___COLORADO AMBUSH ....MON ....1951.....JOHNNY MACK BROWN
___BLAZING BULLETS ....MON ....1951.....JOHNNY MACK BROWN
___TEXAS LAWMEN ....MON ....1951.....JOHNNY MACK BROWN
___TEXAS CITY......................................MON ....1952.....JOHNNY MACK BROWN
___NIGHT RAIDERS ....MON ....1952.....WHIP WILSON
___CHEROKEE UPRISING.....................MON ....1952.....WHIP WILSON

RUTH HALL

___DYNAMITE ....WW ......1932.....KEN MAYNARD
___RIDE HIM COWBOY.........................WB ....1932.....JOHN WAYNE
___BETWEEN FIGHTING MEN ....WW ......1932.....KEN MAYNARD
___FLAMING GUNS ....UNI........1932.....TOM MIX
___THE MAN FROM MONTERREY ......WB ....1933.....JOHN WAYNE
___THE STRAWBERRY ROAN ....UNI........1933.....KEN MAYNARD

MARIE HARMON

___SPRINGTIME IN TEXAS ....MON ....1945.....JIMMY WAKELY
___EL PASO KID ....REP .....1946.....SUNSET CARSON
___NIGHTTIME IN NEVADA..................REP .....1948.....ROY ROGERS
___GUNSMOKE ....AST......1947.....NICK STUART

MARIA HART

___THE FIGHTING STALLION ....EL ....1950.....BILL EDWARDS
___BORDER OUTLAWS ....EL ....1950.....BILL EDWARDS
___OUTLAW WOMEN ....HOW ....1952.....MARIE WINDSOR

SARAH HAYDEN

___RODEO ....MON ....1952.....JANE NIGH
___WAGONS WEST ....MON ....1952.....ROD CAMERON
___TWO-GUN MARSHAL ....UA ....1953.....GUY MADISON

BERNADENE HAYES

___THE JUDGEMENT BOOK ....BEA .....1935.....CONWAY TEARLE
___TRIGGER TOM ....REL......1935.....TOM TYLER
___NORTH OF THE RIO GRANDE ....PAR .....1937.....WILLIAM BOYD
___RUSTLERS' VALLEY.........................PAR .....1937.....WILLIAM BOYD
___SANTA FE MARSHAL ....PAR .....1940.....WILLIAM BOYD

LINDA HAYES

___MEN OF THE TIMBERLAND............UNI ......1941.....RICHARD ARLEN
___SOUTH OF SANTA FE ....REP .....1942.....ROY ROGERS
___ROMANCE ON THE RANGE ....REP .....1942.....ROY ROGERS
___RIDING DOWN THE CANYON ....REP .....1942.....ROY ROGERS

RITA HAYWORTH (RITA CANSINO)

___UNDER A PAMPAS MOON..............FOX .....1935.....WARNER BAXTER
___REBELLION.......................................RKO.....1936.....TOM KEENE
___OLD LOUISIANA ....CRE .....1937.....TOM KEENE
___HIT THE SADDLE ....REP .....1937.....LIVINGSTON/CORRIGAN
___TROUBLE IN TEXAS ....GN ....1937.....TEX RITTER
___THE RENEGADE RANGER ....RKO.....1938.....GEORGE O'BRIEN

GLORIA HENRY

___ADVENTURE IN SILVERADO ....COL .....1948.....WILLIAM BISHOP
___STRAWBERRY ROAN.......................COL .....1948.....GENE AUTRY
___LAW OF THE BARBARY COAST ....COL .....1949.....STEPHEN DUNNE
___RIDERS IN THE SKY........................COL .....1949.....GENE AUTRY
___INDIAN TERRITORY ....COL .....1950.....GENE AUTRY
___LIGHTNING GUNS ....COL .....1950.....CHARLES STARRETT
___AL JENNINGS OF OKLAHOMA.......COL .....1951.....DAN DURYEA

VIRGINIA HERRICK

___VIGILANTE HIDEOUT ....REP .....1950.....ALLAN LANE
___I KILLED GERONIMO........................LIP ....1950.....JAMES ELLISON
___SILVER RAIDERS............................MON ....1950.....WHIP WILSON
___OUTLAW GOLD ....MON ....1950.....JOHNNY MACK BROWN
___MONTANA DESPERADO.................MON ....1951.....JOHNNY MACK BROWN
___FRONTIER PHANTOM ....WA ....1952.....LASH LARUE

DORIS HILL

___SONG OF THE CABALLERO...........UNI ......1930.....KEN MAYNARD

___SONS OF THE SADDLE ....UNI.......1930.....KEN MAYNARD
___CODE OF HONOR ....SYN .....1930.....MAHLON HAMILTON
___THE MONTANA KID ....MON ....1931.....BILL CODY
___ONE WAY TRAIL ....COL .....1931.....TIM McCOY
___SPIRIT OF THE WEST ....ALL ......1932.....HOOT GIBSON
___SOUTH OF THE RIO GRANDE ....COL .....1932.....BUCK JONES
___BATTLING BUCKAROO ....KEN .....1932.....LANE CHANDLER
___TEXAS TORNADO ....KEN .....1932.....LANE CHANDLER
___VIA PONY EXPRESS ....MAJ......1933.....JACK HOXIE
___CRASHING BROADWAY ....MON ....1933.....REX BELL
___GALLOPING ROMEO ....MON ....1933.....BOB STEELE
___THE RANGERS CODE ....MON ....1933.....BOB STEELE
___TRAILING NORTH ....MON ....1933.....BOB STEELE

JOSEPHINE HILL

___THE APACHE KIDS' ESCAPE ....HP........1930.....JACK PERRIN
___WEST OF CHEYENNE ....SYN .....1931.....TOM TYLER
___WILD WEST WHOOPEE ....COS .....1931.....JACK PERRIN
___THE KID FROM ARIZONA ....COS .....1931.....JACK PERRIN
___CHEYENNE CYCLONE ....KEN .....1932.....LANE CHANDLER
___THE LONE TRAIL ....SYN .....1932.....REX LEASE
___POTLUCK PARDS ....REL......1934.....WALLY WALES

VERNA HILLIE

___UNDER THE TONTO RIM ....PAR .....1933.....STU ERWIN
___MAN OF THE FOREST ....PAR .....1933.....RANDOLPH SCOTT
___THE STAR PACKER ....MON ....1934.....JOHN WAYNE
___THE TRAIL BEYOND ....MON ....1934.....JOHN WAYNE

GERTRUDE HOFFMAN

___CASSIDY OF BAR 20 ....PAR .....1938.....WILLIAM BOYD
___NORTH OF THE ROCKIES..............COL .....1942.....ELLIOTT/RITTER
___TEXAS TROUBLE SHOOTERS ....MON ....1942.....CORRIGAN/KING

JENNIFER HOLT

___STICK TO YOUR GUNS ....PAR .....1941.....WILLIAM BOYD
___THE SILVER BULLET.......................UNI.......1942.....JOHNNY MACK BROWN
___DEEP IN THE HEART OF TEXAS ...UNI.......1942.....BROWN/RITTER
___LITTLE JOE, THE WRANGLER ....UNI.......1942.....BROWN/RITTER
___THE OLD CHISHOLM TRAIL ....UNI.......1942.....BROWN/RITTER
___TENTING TONIGHT ON THE OLD..UNI.......1943.....BROWN/RITTER
CAMPGROUND
___CHEYENNE ROUNDUP ....UNI.......1943.....BROWN/RITTER
___RAIDERS OF SAN JOAQUIN...........UNI.......1943.....BROWN/RITTER
___LONE STAR TRAIL...........................UNI.......1943.....BROWN/RITTER

___FRONTIER LAW ....UNI ......1943.....RUSSELL HAYDEN
___RAIDERS OF SUNSET PASS..........REP .....1943.....EDDIE DEW
___MARSHAL OF GUNSMOKE.............UNI ......1944.....TEX RITTER
___OKLAHOMA RAIDERS ....UNI ......1944.....TEX RITTER
___GUNS OF THE LAW ....PRC .....1944.....NEWILL/O'BRIEN
___OUTLAW TRAIL ....MON ....1944.....GIBSON/STEELE
___RIDERS OF THE SANTA FE ....UNI ......1944.....ROD CAMERON
___THE NAVAJO TRAIL ....MON ....1945.....JOHNNY MACK BROWN
___THE LAST TRAIL ....MON ....1945.....JOHNNY MACK BROWN
___BEYOND THE PECOS ....UNI ......1945.....ROD CAMERON
___RENEGADES OF THE RIO GRANDE .UNI ......1945.....ROD CAMERON
___SONG OF OLD WYOMING ....PRC .....1945.....EDDIE DEAN
___UNDER WESTERN SKIES...............UNI ......1945.....NOAH BERRY, JR.
___MOON OVER MONTANA ....MON ....1946.....JIMMY WAKELY
___TRIGGER FINGERS ....MON ....1946.....JOHNNY MACK BROWN
___OVER THE SANTA FE TRAIL..........COL .....1947.....KEN CURTIS
___GUNSMOKE.....................................MON ....1947.....JOHNNY MACK BROWN
___BUFFALO BILL RIDES AGAIN ....SG ....1947.....RICHARD ARLEN
___PIONEER JUSTICE ....PRC .....1947.....LASH LARUE
___GHOST TOWN RENEGADES..........PRC .....1947.....LASH LARUE
___FIGHTING VIGILANTES...................PRC .....1947.....LASH LARUE

Jennifer Holt with Gil Patrick and Richard Arien

___SHADOW VALLEY .... PRC ..... 1947 ..... EDDIE DEAN
___HAWK OF POWDER RIVER .... PRC ..... 1948 ..... EDDIE DEAN
___RANGE RENEGADES .... MON .... 1948 ..... JIMMY WAKELY
___STAGE TO MESA CITY .... PRC ..... 1948 ..... LASH LARUE
___WHERE THE NORTH BEGINS .... SG .... 1948 ..... RUSSELL HAYDEN
___TRAIL OF THE MOUNTIES .... SG .... 1948 ..... RUSSELL HAYDEN
___TORNADO RANGE .... EL .... 1948 ..... EDDIE DEAN
___TIOGA KID .... EL .... 1948 ..... EDDIE DEAN

DORIS HOUCK

___TWO-FISTED STRANGER .... COL ..... 1946 ..... CHARLES STARRETT
___HEADING WEST .... COL ..... 1946 ..... CHARLES STARRETT
___LANDRUSH .... COL ..... 1946 ..... CHARLES STARRETT

Doris Houck with Smiley Burnette

ANN HOWARD

___LAWLESS VALLEY .... KEN ..... 1932 ..... LANE CHANDLER
___CRASHING BROADWAY .... MON .... 1933 ..... REX BELL
___THE FIGHTING TEXAN .... MON .... 1933 ..... REX BELL

___LIGHTNING RANGE ....SPR ..... 1934 ..... BUDDY ROOSEVELT
___ARIZONA BADMAN ....KEN ..... 1935 ..... REB RUSSELL
___TOMBSTONE TERROR ....SUP ..... 1935 ..... BOB STEELE

ROCHELLE HUDSON

___BEYOND THE ROCKIES ....RKO ..... 1932 ..... TOM KEENE
___THE COUNTRY BEYOND ....FOX ..... 1936 ..... PAUL KELLY
___KONGA-THE WILD STALLION ....COL ..... 1940 ..... FRED STONE

CAROL HUGHES

___RENFREW OF THE ROYAL MOUNTED ....GN .... 1937 ..... JIM NEWILL
___UNDER WESTERN STARS ....REP ..... 1938 ..... ROY ROGERS
___GOLD MINE IN THE SKY ....REP ..... 1938 ..... GENE AUTRY
___MAN FROM MUSIC MOUNTAIN .....REP ..... 1938 ..... GENE AUTRY
___THE BORDER LEGION ....REP ..... 1940 ..... ROY ROGERS

Carol Hughes with Jim Newill

___UNDER FIESTA STARS ....REP .....1941.....GENE AUTRY
___HOME IN OKLAHOMA......................REP .....1946.....ROY ROGERS
___THE STAGECOACH KID ....RKO .....1949.....TIM HOLT

KAY HUGHES

___THE THREE MESQUITEERS ....REP .....1936.....LIVINGSTON/CORRIGAN
___RIDE, RANGER, RIDE......................REP .....1936.....GENE AUTRY
___GHOST TOWN GOLD ....REP .....1936.....LIVINGSTON/CORRIGAN
___THE BIG SHOW ....REP .....1936.....GENE AUTRY
___RIDERS OF THE BADLANDS..........COL .....1941.....CHARLES STARRETT
___ENEMY OF THE LAW......................PRC .....1945.....RITTER/O'BRIEN
___FIGHTING BILL CARSON ....PRC .....1945.....BUSTER CRABBE

MARY BETH HUGHES

___LUCKY CISCO KID ....20F.......1940.....CESAR ROMERO
___THE COWBOY AND THE BLOND ...20F.......1941.....GEORGE MONTGOMERY
___RIDE ON VAQUERO ....20F.......1941.....CESAR ROMERO
___ROCKIN' IN THE ROCKIES ....COL .....1945.....JAY KIRBY
___LAST OF THE WILD HORSES ....SG........1948.....JAMES ELLISON
___THE RETURN OF WILDFIRE...........SG........1948.....RICHARD ARLEN
___RIMFIRE ....SG........1949.....JAMES MILLICAN
___RIDERS IN THE SKY.......................COL .....1949.....GENE AUTRY
___SQUARE DANCE JUBILEE.............LIP ....1949.....DON BARRY

MARSHA HUNT

___DESERT GOLD ....PAR .....1936.....TOM KEENE
___THE ARIZONA RAIDERS ....PAR .....1936.....BUSTER CRABBE
___THUNDER TRAIL............................PAR .....1937.....GILBERT ROLAND
___BORN TO THE WEST ....PAR .....1937.....JOHNNY MACK BROWN

VIRGINIA HUNTER

___SMOKEY RIVER SERENADE..........COL .....1947.....PAUL CAMPBELL
___THE STRANGER FROM PONCA ....COL .....1947.....CHARLES STARRETT
CITY
___RIDERS OF THE LONE STAR.........COL .....1947.....CHARLES STARRETT
___LAST DAYS OF BOOT HILL ....COL .....1947.....CHARLES STARRETT
___PHANTOM VALLEY ....COL .....1948.....CHARLES STARRETT

MARTHA HYER

___THUNDER MOUNTAIN......................RKO .....1947.....TIM HOLT
___GUN SMUGGLERS..........................RKO .....1948.....TIM HOLT
___RUSTLERS ....RKO .....1949.....TIM HOLT
___OUTCASTS OF BLACK MESA ....COL .....1950.....CHARLES STARRETT
___SALT LAKE RAIDERS ....REP .....1950.....ALLAN LANE
___FRISCO TORNADO ....REP .....1950.....ALLAN LANE

___YUKON GOLD .... MON .... 1952..... KIRBY GRANT
___WILD STALLION .... MON .... 1952..... BEN JOHNSON
___BATTLE OF ROGUE RIVER .... COL ..... 1954..... GEORGE MONTGOMERY

EILENE JANSSEN

___BUCKAROO SHERIFF OF TEXAS .. REP ..... 1951 ..... MICHAEL CHAPIN
___THE DAKOTA KID .... REP ..... 1951 ..... MICHAEL CHAPIN
___ARIZONA MANHUNT .... REP ..... 1951 ..... MICHAEL CHAPIN
___RANGERS OF THE GOLDEN SAGE REP ..... 1951 ..... MICHAEL CHAPIN
___WILD HORSE AMBUSH .... REP ..... 1951 ..... MICHAEL CHAPIN

LOIS JANUARY

___ARIZONA BAD MAN .... KEN ..... 1935..... REB RUSSELL
___SKULL AND CROWN .... REL...... 1935..... RIN TIN TIN
___BORDER CABALLERO .... PUR ..... 1936..... TIM McCOY
___LIGHTNIN' BILL CARSON .... PUR ..... 1936..... TIM McCOY
___ROGUE OF THE RANGE .... REP ..... 1936..... JOHNNY MACK BROWN
___LIGHTNIN' CRANDALL .... REP ..... 1937..... BOB STEELE
___BAR Z BAD MAN .... REP ..... 1937..... JOHNNY MACK BROWN
___THE TRUSTED OUTLAW.................. REP ..... 1937..... BOB STEELE
___THE RED ROPE................................ REP ..... 1937..... BOB STEELE

Lois January with Johnny Mack Brown

___COURAGE OF THE WEST ....UNI.......1937.....BOB BAKER
___MOONLIGHT ON THE RANGE........SPE .....1937.....FRED SCOTT
___THE ROAMING COWBOY ....SPE .....1937.....FRED SCOTT

ANNE JEFFREYS

___BILLY THE KID TRAPPED ....PRC .....1942.....BUSTER CRABBE
___CALLING WILD BILL ELLIOTT ....REP .....1943.....BILL ELLIOTT
___MAN FROM THUNDER RIVER........REP .....1943.....BILL ELLIOTT
___DEATH VALLEY MANHUNT ....REP .....1943.....BILL ELLIOTT
___BORDERTOWN GUNFIGHTER.......REP .....1943.....BILL ELLIOTT
___WAGON TRACKS WEST ....REP .....1943.....BILL ELLIOTT
___OVERLAND MAIL ROBBERY ....REP .....1943.....BILL ELLIOTT
___MOJAVE FIREBRAND......................REP .....1944.....BILL ELLIOTT
___HIDDEN VALLEY OUTLAWS...........REP .....1944.....BILL ELLIOTT
___NEVADA ....RKO .....1944.....ROBERT MITCHUM
___TRAIL STREET ....RKO .....1947.....RANDOLPH SCOTT
___RETURN OF THE BADMAN ....RKO .....1948.....RANDOLPH SCOTT

JUNE JOHNSON

___THE BIG SHOW ....REP .....1936.....GENE AUTRY
___LONE STAR RAIDERS ....REP .....1940.....LIVINGSTON/STEELE
___PALS OF THE PECOS ....REP .....1941.....LIVINGSTON/STEELE
___GANGS OF SONORA ....REP .....1941.....LIVINGSTON/STEELE

LINDA JOHNSON

___SUNDOWN KID ....REP .....1942.....DON BARRY
___WILD HORSE RUSTLERS ....PRC .....1943.....BOB LIVINGSTON
___HAUNTED MINE ....MON ....1946.....JOHNNY MACK BROWN
___BANDITS OF DARK CANYON ....REP .....1947.....ALLAN LANE

BEVERLY JONS

___RIDIN' DOWN THE TRAIL................MON ....1947.....JIMMY WAKELY
___CARSON CITY RAIDERS.................REP .....1948.....ALLAN LANE
___THE GAY AMIGO.............................UA........1949.....DUNCAN RENALDO

JEAN JOYCE

___OUTLAWS OF SONORA..................REP .....1938.....LIVINGSTON/CORRIGAN
___RIDERS OF THE FRONTIER...........MON ....1939.....TEX RITTER
___OVERLAND MAIL ....MON ....1939.....JACK RANDALL

NAOMI JUDGE

___THE MAN FROM ARIZONA ....MON ....1932.....REX BELL
___YOUNG BLOOD ....MON ....1932.....BOB STEELE
___TERROR TRAIL ....UNI.......1933.....TOM MIX

BERNICE KAY (CARA WILLIAMS)

___WIDE OPEN TOWN ....PAR ..... 1941 ..... WILLIAM BOYD
___SADDLE PALS ....REP ..... 1946 ..... GENE AUTRY
___MARSHAL OF AMARILLO ....REP ..... 1948 ..... ALLAN LANE

MARY ELLEN KAY

___STREETS OF GHOST TOWN ....COL ..... 1950 ..... CHARLES STARRETT
___SILVER CITY BONANZA ....REP ..... 1951 ..... REX ALLEN
___THUNDER IN GODS' COUNTRY ....REP ..... 1951 ..... REX ALLEN
___WELLS FARGO GUNMASTER ....REP ..... 1951 ..... ALLAN LANE

Anne Jeffreys with "Wild" Bill Elliott and George "Gabby" Hayes

___RODEO KING AND THE SENORITA REP ..... 1951 ..... REX ALLEN
___FORT DODGE STAMPEDE ....REP ..... 1951 ..... ALLAN LANE
___DESERT OF LOST MEN ....REP ..... 1951 ..... ALLAN LANE
___COLORADO SUNDOWN ....REP ..... 1951 ..... REX ALLEN
___THE LAST MUSKETEER....................REP ..... 1952 ..... REX ALLEN
___BORDER SADDLEMATES ....REP ..... 1952 ..... REX ALLEN
___VIGILANTE TERROR ....AA .... 1953 ..... BILL ELLIOTT
___YUKON VENGEANCE ....AA .... 1954 ..... KIRBY GRANT

JANE KECKLEY

___THE TONTO KID ....RES ..... 1935 ..... REX BELL

___ROARING LEAD ....REP .....1936.....LIVINGSTON/CORRIGAN
___SIX SHOOTING SHERIFF................GN ....1938.....KEN MAYNARD
___LIGHTNING CARSON RIDES AGAIN VIC.......1938.....TIM McCOY
___IN OLD MONTANA ....SPE .....1939.....FRED SCOTT

ROSALIND KEITH

___KING OF THE ROYAL MOUNTED ..20T.......1936.....ROBERT KENT
___WESTBOUND MAIL..........................COL .....1937.....CHARLES STARRETT
___TROUBLE IN SUNDOWN.................RKO.....1939.....GEORGE O'BRIEN

JEANNE KELLY (JEAN BROOKS)

___SON OF ROARING DAN ....UNI.......1941.....JOHNNY MACK BROWN
___MAN FROM MONTANA....................UNI.......1941.....JOHNNY MACK BROWN
___FIGHTING BILL FARGO...................UNI.......1941.....JOHNNY MACK BROWN
___BOOTHILL BANDITS ....MON ....1942.....CORRIGAN/KING

MERNA KENNEDY

___THE GAY BUCKAROO.....................ALL ......1932.....HOOT GIBSON
___GHOST VALLEY ....RKO .....1932.....TOM KEENE
___COME ON TARZAN ....WW ......1932.....KEN MAYNARD

DOROTHEA KENT

___DANGER AHEAD ....MON ....1940.....JAMES NEWILL
___CALL OF THE CANYON...................REP .....1942.....GENE AUTRY
___KING OF THE COWBOYS ....REP .....1943.....ROY ROGERS

EVELYN KNAPP

___THE VANISHING FRONTIER...........PAR .....1932.....JOHNNY MACK BROWN
___IN OLD SANTA FE ....MAS .....1934.....KEN MAYNARD
___HAWAIIAN BUCKAROO...................20T.......1938.....SMITH BALLEW
___RAWHIDE ....20T.......1938.....SMITH BALLEW

LYDIA KNOTT

___OVERLAND BOUND.........................RAY .....1929.....LEO MALONEY
___MEN WITHOUT LAW........................COL .....1930.....BUCK JONES
___ROCKY RHODES ....UNI.......1934.....BUCK JONES

PATRICIA KNOX

___THE LONE RIDER IN BORDER.......PRC .....1943.....GEORGE HOUSTON
ROUNDUP
___TRAIL OF TERROR ....PRC .....1943.....NEWILL/O'BRIEN
___FLAMING BULLETS ....PRC .....1945.....RITTER/O'BRIEN
___GENTLEMEN WITH GUNS ....PRC .....1946.....BUSTER CRABBE
___PRAIRIE BADMEN...........................PRC .....1946.....BUSTER CRABBE
___SINGING SPURS ....COL .....1948.....KIRBY GRANT

ADELE LACY (TRACY)

___VANISHING MEN .... MON .... 1932..... TOM TYLER
___WYOMING WHIRLWIND .... KEN ..... 1932..... LANE CHANDLER
___WHEN A MAN RIDES ALONE .... FM .... 1933..... TOM TYLER

FLORENCE LAKE

___FARGO .... MON .... 1952..... BILL ELLIOTT
___THE MAVERICK .... AA .... 1952..... BILL ELLIOTT
___MAN FROM THE BLACK HILLS ...... MON .... 1952..... JOHNNY MACK BROWN
___BITTER CREEK .... AA .... 1954..... BILL ELLIOTT
___THE DESPERADO .... AA .... 1954..... WAYNE MORRIS

NORA LANE

___LUCKY LARKIN .... UNI ...... 1930..... KEN MAYNARD
___THE CISCO KID .... FOX ..... 1931..... WARNER BAXTER
___THE WESTERN CODE .... COL ..... 1932..... TIM McCOY
___OUTLAW DEPUTY .... PUR ..... 1935..... TIM McCOY
___WESTERN FRONTIER .... COL ..... 1935..... KEN MAYNARD
___WESTERN JUSTICE .... SUP ..... 1936..... BOB STEELE
___BORDERLAND .... PAR ..... 1937..... WILLIAM BOYD
___HOPALONG RIDES AGAIN .... PAR ..... 1937..... WILLIAM BOYD
___WEST OF RAINBOWS END .... MON .... 1938..... TIM McCOY
___CASSIDY OF BAR 20 .... PAR ..... 1938..... WILLIAM BOYD
___SIX GUN TRAIL .... VIC .... 1938..... TIM McCOY
___TEXAS RENEGADES .... PRC ..... 1940..... TIM McCOY
___HEART OF THE RIO GRANDE .... REP ..... 1942..... GENE AUTRY
___UNDERCOVER MAN .... UA .... 1942..... WILLIAM BOYD

CARMEN LAROUX

___CAVALIER OF THE WEST .... ART ..... 1931..... HARRY CAREY
___TWO GUN CABALLERO .... IMP ...... 1931..... ROBERT FRAZER
___SON OF OKLAHOMA .... WW ...... 1932..... BOB STEELE
___THE CALIFORNIA TRAIL .... COL ..... 1933..... BUCK JONES
___A DEMON FOR TROUBLE .... SUP ..... 1934..... BOB STEELE
___THE DESERT TRAIL .... MON .... 1935..... JOHN WAYNE
___CHEYENNE RIDES AGAIN .... VIC .... 1937..... TOM TYLER
___STARLIGHT OVER TEXAS .... MON .... 1938..... TEX RITTER

CHRISTINE LARSON

___RANGE RENEGADES .... MON .... 1948..... JIMMY WAKELY
___THE FIGHTING RANGER .... MON .... 1948..... JOHNNY MACK BROWN
___PARTNERS OF THE SUNSET .... MON .... 1948..... JIMMY WAKELY
___SILVER TRAILS .... MON .... 1948..... JIMMY WAKELY
___OUTLAW BRAND .... MON .... 1948..... JIMMY WAKELY
___HIDDEN DANGER .... MON .... 1948..... JOHNNY MACK BROWN

___CRASHING THRU .... MON .... 1949 ..... WHIP WILSON
___VALLEY OF FIRE .... COL ..... 1951 ..... GENE AUTRY

MADY LAWRENCE

___HEART OF THE RIO GRANDE .... REP ..... 1942 ..... GENE AUTRY
___PINTO BANDIT .... PRC .... 1944 ..... NEWILL/O'BRIEN
___SPOOK TOWN .... PRC ..... 1944 ..... NEWILL/O'BRIEN
___OATH OF VENGEANCE .... PRC ..... 1944 ..... BUSTER CRABBE
___LIGHTNING RAIDERS .... PRC ..... 1945 ..... BUSTER CRABBE

MARY LEE

___SOUTH OF THE BORDER .... REP ..... 1939 ..... GENE AUTRY
___RANCHO GRANDE .... REP ..... 1940 ..... GENE AUTRY
___GAUCHO SERENADE .... REP ..... 1940 ..... GENE AUTRY
___CAROLINA MOON .... REP ..... 1940 ..... GENE AUTRY
___RIDE TENDERFOOT, RIDE .... REP ..... 1940 ..... GENE AUTRY
___MELODY RANCH .... REP ..... 1940 ..... GENE AUTRY
___RIDING ON A RAINBOW .... REP ..... 1941 ..... GENE AUTRY
___BACK IN THE SADDLE .... REP ..... 1941 ..... GENE AUTRY
___MEET ROY ROGERS .... REP ..... 1941 ..... ROY ROGERS
___THE SINGING HILL .... REP ..... 1941 ..... GENE AUTRY
___THE COWBOY AND THE SENORITA . REP ..... 1944 ..... ROY ROGERS
___SONG OF NEVADA .... REP ..... 1944 ..... ROY ROGERS

RUTH LEE

___TUCSON RAIDERS .... REP ..... 1944 ..... BILL ELLIOTT
___CORPUS CHRISTI BANDITS .... REP ..... 1945 ..... ALLAN LANE
___THE DALTONS RIDE AGAIN .... UNI .... 1945 ..... ALAN CURTIS

MAXINE LESLIE

___RIDERS OF THE FRONTIER .... MON .... 1939 ..... TEX RITTER
___OVERLAND MAIL .... MON .... 1939 ..... JACK RANDALL
___THE LONE RIDER AMBUSHED ...... PRC ..... 1941 ..... GEORGE HOUSTON
___SHERIFF OF SAGE VALLEY .... PRC ..... 1942 ..... BUSTER CRABBE
___FUGITIVE OF THE PLAINS .... PRC ..... 1943 ..... BUSTER CRABBE

NAN LESLIE

___SUNSET PASS .... RKO ..... 1946 ..... JAMES WARREN
___UNDER THE TONTO RIM .... RKO ..... 1947 ..... TIM HOLT
___WILD HORSE MESA .... RKO ..... 1947 ..... TIM HOLT
___WESTERN HERITAGE .... RKO ..... 1948 ..... TIM HOLT
___GUNS OF HATE .... RKO ..... 1948 ..... TIM HOLT
___THE ARIZONA RANGER .... RKO ..... 1948 ..... TIM HOLT
___INDIAN AGENT .... RKO ..... 1948 ..... TIM HOLT
___RIM OF THE CANYON .... COL ..... 1949 ..... GENE AUTRY

___PIONEER MARSHAL........................REP .....1949.....MONTE HALE
___TRAIN TO TOMBSTONE..................LIP ....1950.....DON BARRY
___IRON MOUNTAIN TRAIL..................REP .....1953.....REX ALLEN

Nan Leslie with Robert Bray and Myrna Dell

CARYL LINCOLN

___THE LAND OF MISSING MEN ....TIF ....1930.....BOB STEELE
___THE CYCLONE KID...........................B4 ....1931.....BUZZ BARTON
___QUICK TRIGGER LEE.......................B4 ....1931.....BOB CUSTER
___THE MAN FROM NEW MEXICO .....MON ....1932.....TOM TYLER
___MAN OF ACTION.............................COL .....1933.....TIM McCOY
___WAR ON THE RANGE.......................FM ....1933.....TOM TYLER

AUDREY LONG

___TALL IN THE SADDLE ....RKO.....1944.....JOHN WAYNE
___WANDERER OF THE WASTELAND RKO.....1945.....JAMES WARREN
___CAVALRY SCOUT ....MON ....1951.....ROD CAMERON
___INDIAN UPRISING...........................COL .....1952.....GEORGE MONTGOMERY

MARJORIE LORD

___THE BORDER CAFE ....RKO.....1937.....HARRY CAREY
___THE MASKED RAIDERS..................RKO.....1949.....TIM HOLT
___REBEL CITY.....................................AA ....1953.....BILL ELLIOTT
___DOWN LAREDO WAY ....REP .....1953.....REX ALLEN

LOUISE LORRAINE

___THE MOUNTED STRANGER...........UNI ......1930.....HOOT GIBSON
___NEAR THE RAINBOW'S END..........TIF ....1930.....BOB STEELE

___BEYOND THE LAW ....SYN .....1930.....ROBERT FRAZER

ELLEN LOWE

___RANCHO GRANDE.............................REP .....1940.....GENE AUTRY
___WAGON TRAIN ....RKO .....1940.....TIM HOLT
___SADDLEMATES ....REP .....1941.....LIVINGSTON/STEELE
___BORDERTOWN TRAIL.......................REP .....1944.....SUNSET CARSON

MYRNA LOY

___LAST OF THE DUANES ....FOX .....1930.....GEORGE O'BRIEN
___THE BAD MAN ....FN ....1930.....WALTER HUSTON
___ROGUE OF THE RIO GRANDE.......WW ......1930.....JOSE BOHR

LUCILLE LUND

___FIGHTING THRU ....KEN .....1934.....REB RUSSELL
___RANGE WARFARE.............................KEN .....1935.....REB RUSSELL
___TIMBER WAR ....AMB .....1935.....KERMIT MAYNARD
___RIO GRANDE ROMANCE ....VIC ....1936.....EDDIE NUGENT

BETTY MACK

___GODS' COUNTRY AND THE MAN..SYN .....1931.....TOM TYLER
___PARTNERS OF THE TRAIL ....MON ....1931.....TOM TYLER
___LAW OF THE RIO GRANDE ....SYN .....1931.....BOB CUSTER
___MAN FROM DEATH VALLEY...........MON ....1931.....TOM TYLER
___HEADIN FOR TROUBLE ....B4 ....1931.....BOB CUSTER
___SCARLET BRAND ....B4 ....1932.....BOB CUSTER
___THE FORTY NINERS ....FM........1932.....TOM TYLER
___GALLOPING THROUGH ....MON ....1932.....TOM TYLER
___THE FIGHTING TEXANS ....MON ....1933.....REX BELL
___OUTLAW RULE.................................KEN .....1935.....REB RUSSELL
___THE LAST OF THE CLINTONS ....AJA ......1935.....HARRY CAREY
___RECKLESS BUCKAROO ....CRE .....1935.....BILL CODY
___TOLL OF THE DESERT ....COM ....1935.....FRED KOHLER, JR.
___HAIR TRIGGER CASEY ....ATL ......1936.....JACK PERRIN
___SENOR JIM ....BEA .....1936.....CONWAY TEARLE
___ROUGH RIDING RHYTHM...............AMB .....1937.....KERMIT MAYNARD
___THE PAL FROM TEXAS...................MET .....1939.....BOB STEELE

DOROTHY MALONE

___FRONTIER DAYS ....WB ....1945.....ROBERT SHAYNE
___SADDLE LEGION..............................RKO .....1951.....TIM HOLT
___THE LONE GUN ....UA ....1954.....GEORGE MONTGOMERY

MARJORIE MANNERS

___TUMBLEWEED TRAIL......................PRC .....1942.....BOYD/DAVIS

___TEXAS TO BATAAN .... MON .... 1942..... KING/SHARPE
___OUTLAWS OF BOULDER PASS ..... PRC ..... 1942..... GEORGE HOUSTON
___WESTERN CYCLONE .... PRC ..... 1943..... BUSTER CRABBE
___BLAZING FRONTIER .... PRC ..... 1943..... BUSTER CRABBE
___FRONTIER FUGITIVES .... PRC ..... 1945..... BUSTER CRABBE

SHEILA MANNORS (SHELIA LEGAY, SHEILA BROMLEY)

___CALL OF THE DESERT .... SYN ..... 1930..... TOM TYLER
___CANYON OF MISSING MEN .... SYN ..... 1930..... TOM TYLER
___TEXAS GUNFIGHTER .... TIF .... 1932..... KEN MAYNARD
___TEXAS PIONEERS .... MON .... 1932..... BILL CODY
___THE COWBOY COUNSELOR .... ALL ...... 1932..... HOOT GIBSON
___LAND OF WANTED MEN .... MON .... 1932..... BILL CODY
___THE PRESCOTT KID .... COL ..... 1932..... TIM McCOY
___WESTWARD HO .... REP ..... 1935..... JOHN WAYNE
___MOONLIGHT ON THE PRAIRIE ...... WB .... 1935..... DICK FORAN
___LAWLESS RANGE .... REP ..... 1935..... JOHN WAYNE
___DESERT PHANTOM .... SUP ..... 1936..... JOHNNY MACK BROWN

Sheila Mannors with John Wayne

ADELE MARA

___VENGEANCE OF THE WEST .... COL ..... 1941..... ELLIOTT/RITTER
___RIDERS OF THE NORTHWEST ...... COL ..... 1943..... RUSSELL HAYDEN
MOUNTED

___SONG OF MEXICO .... REP ..... 1945 ..... EDGAR BARRIER
___BELLS OF ROSARITA .... REP ..... 1945 ..... ROY ROGERS
___TWILIGHT ON THE RIO GRANDE .. REP ..... 1947 ..... GENE AUTRY
___ROBIN HOOD OF TEXAS .... REP ..... 1947 ..... GENE AUTRY
___GALLANT LEGION .... REP ..... 1948 ..... BILL ELLIOTT
___NIGHT TIME IN NEVADA .... REP ..... 1948 ..... ROY ROGERS
___CALIFORNIA PASSAGE .... REP ..... 1950 ..... FORREST TUCKER
___ROCK ISLAND TRAIL .... REP ..... 1950 ..... FORREST TUCKER

BETH MARION (BETTY LLOYD)

___BETWEEN MEN .... SUP ..... 1935 ..... JOHNNY MACK BROWN
___TRAIL OF TERROR .... SUP ..... 1935 ..... BOB STEELE
___SILVER SPURS .... UNI .... 1936 ..... BUCK JONES
___FOR THE SERVICE .... UNI .... 1936 ..... BUCK JONES
___EVERYMANS' LAW .... SUP ..... 1936 ..... JOHNNY MACK BROWN
___AVENGING WATERS .... COL ..... 1936 ..... KEN MAYNARD
___RIP ROARING BUCKAROO .... VIC .... 1936 ..... TOM TYLER
___THE FUGITIVE SHERIFF .... COL ..... 1936 ..... KEN MAYNARD
___PHANTOM OF THE RANGE .... VIC .... 1936 ..... TOM TYLER
___WILD HORSE ROUNDUP .... AMB ..... 1936 ..... KERMIT MAYNARD
___PHANTOM GOLD .... COL ..... 1938 ..... JACK LUDEN
___FRONTIER SCOUT .... GN .... 1938 ..... GEORGE HOUSTON

Beth Marion with Ken Maynard

MARGARET MARQUIS

___LAST OF THE WARRENS ....SUP ..... 1936..... BOB STEELE
___BRAND OF THE OUTLAWS ....SUP ..... 1936..... BOB STEELE
___CASSIDY OF BAR 20 ....PAR ..... 1938..... WILLIAM BOYD

NINA MARTAN

___BORDER ROMANCE ....TIF .... 1930..... ARMIDA
___UNDER MONTANA SKIES ....TIF .... 1930..... KENNETH HARLAN
___THE TWO GUN MAN ....TIF .... 1931..... KEN MAYNARD

JEANNE MARTEL

___SANTA FE BOUND ....REL...... 1936..... TOM TYLER
___ORPHAN OF THE PECOS ....VIC .... 1937..... TOM TYLER
___LOST RANCH ....VIC .... 1937..... TOM TYLER

JUNE MARTEL

___ARIZONA MAHONEY ....PAR ..... 1936..... BUSTER CRABBE
___FORLORN RIVER ....PAR ..... 1937..... BUSTER CRABBE
___WILD HORSE RODEO ....REP ..... 1937..... LIVINGSTON/CORRIGAN
___SANTA FE STAMPEDE ....REP ..... 1938..... WAYNE/CORRIGAN

DONNA MARTELL

___TWILIGHT ON THE RIO GRANDE .. REP ..... 1947..... GENE AUTRY
___TALES OF THE WEST ....UNI ...... 1950..... TEX WILLIAMS
___HILLS OF UTAH ....COL ..... 1951..... GENE AUTRY

JANET MARTIN

___HANDS ACROSS THE BORDER .... REP ..... 1944..... ROY ROGERS
___YELLOW ROSE OF TEXAS ....REP ..... 1944..... ROY ROGERS
___BELLS OF ROSARITA.......................REP ..... 1945..... ROY ROGERS

CAROLE MATTHEWS

___SWING IN THE SADDLE...................COL ..... 1944..... JANE FRAZEE
___BLAZING THE WESTERN TRAIL .... COL ..... 1945..... CHARLES STARRETT
___OUTLAWS OF THE ROCKIES ....COL ..... 1945..... CHARLES STARRETT
___SING ME A SONG OF TEXAS ....COL ..... 1945..... TOM TYLER
___TWO-GUN MARSHAL ....AA .... 1953..... GUY MADISON

PATTI McCARTY

___PRAIRIE STRANGER ....COL ..... 1941..... CHARLES STARRETT
___FIGHTING VALLEY...........................PRC ..... 1943..... NEWILL/O'BRIEN
___DEVIL RIDERS.....................................PRC ..... 1943..... BUSTER CRABBE
___GUNSMOKE MESA ....PRC ..... 1944..... NEWILL/O'BRIEN
___FUZZY SETTLES DOWN ....PRC ..... 1944..... BUSTER CRABBE

___RUSTLER'S HIDEOUT .... PRC ..... 1944 ..... BUSTER CRABBE
___GANGSTERS OF THE FRONTIER .. PRC ..... 1944 ..... RITTER/O'BRIEN
___TERRORS ON HORSEBACK .... PRC ..... 1946 ..... BUSTER CRABBE
___OVERLAND RIDERS .... PRC ..... 1946 ..... BUSTER CRABBE
___OUTLAW OF THE PLAINS .... PRC ..... 1946 ..... BUSTER CRABBE

ETTA McDANIEL

___SMOKING GUNS .... UNI .... 1934 ..... KEN MAYNARD
___THE LAWLESS NINETIES .... REP ..... 1936 ..... JOHN WAYNE
___THE LONELY TRAIL .... REP ..... 1936 ..... JOHN WAYNE
___THE GLORY TRAIL .... CRE ..... 1936 ..... TOM KEENE
___CAROLINA MOON .... REP ..... 1940 ..... GENE AUTRY
___AMERICAN EMPIRE .... UA .... 1942 ..... RICHARD DIX

HATTIE McDANIEL

___THE BOILING POINT .... ALL ...... 1932 ..... HOOT GIBSON
___THE GOLDEN WEST .... FOX ..... 1932 ..... GEORGE O'BRIEN
___THE WILDCATTER .... UNI .... 1937 ..... SCOTT COLTON

CLAIRE McDOWELL

___CORNERED .... COL ..... 1933 ..... TIM McCOY
___TWO FISTED SHERIFF .... COL ..... 1937 ..... CHARLES STARRETT
___BLACK MARKET RUSTLERS .... MON .... 1945 ..... RANGE BUSTERS

CHRISTINE McINTYRE

___THE RANGERS ROUNDUP .... SPE ..... 1938 ..... FRED SCOTT
___GUNMAN FROM BODIE .... MON .... 1941 ..... JONES/McCOY
___FORBIDDEN TRAILS .... MON .... 1941 ..... JONES/McCOY
___LAW AND ORDER .... PRC ..... 1942 ..... BUSTER CRABBE
___ROCK RIVER RENEGADES .... MON .... 1942 ..... CORRIGAN/KING
___RIDERS OF THE WEST .... MON .... 1942 ..... JONES/McCOY
___DAWN ON THE GREAT DIVIDE ...... MON .... 1942 ..... BUCK JONES
___BORDER BUCKAROOS .... PRC ..... 1943 ..... NEWILL/O'BRIEN
___THE STRANGER FROM THE PECOS . MON .... 1943 ..... JOHNNY MACK BROWN
___PARTNERS OF THE TRAIL .... MON .... 1944 ..... JOHNNY MACK BROWN
___WEST OF THE RIO GRANDE .... MON .... 1944 ..... JOHNNY MACK BROWN
___FRONTIER FEUD .... MON .... 1945 ..... JOHNNY MACK BROWN
___PISTOL PACKIN' NITWITS .... COL ..... 1945 ..... HARRY LANGDON
___GENTLEMEN FROM TEXAS .... MON .... 1946 ..... JOHNNY MACK BROWN
___THREE TROUBLE DOERS .... COL ..... 1946 ..... THREE STOOGES
___VALLEY OF FEAR .... MON .... 1947 ..... JOHNNY MACK BROWN
___LAND OF THE LAWLESS .... MON .... 1947 ..... JOHNNY MACK BROWN
___GUN TALK .... MON .... 1947 ..... JOHNNY MACK BROWN
___COLORADO AMBUSH .... MON .... 1951 ..... JOHNNY MACK BROWN

	Title	Studio	Year	Star
___	WANTED, DEAD OR ALIVE	MON	1951	WHIP WILSON

WANDA McKAY (TERRY WALKER)

	Title	Studio	Year	Star
___	RENFREW ON THE GREAT WHITE TRAIL	GN	1938	JAMES NEWILL
___	BILLY THE KID IN TEXAS	PRC	1940	BOB STEELE
___	TAKE ME BACK TO OKLAHOMA	MON	1940	TEX RITTER
___	THE PIONEERS	MON	1941	TEX RITTER
___	THE MEDICO OF PAINTED SPRINGS	COL	1941	CHARLES STARRETT
___	TWILIGHT ON THE TRAIL	PAR	1941	WILLIAM BOYD
___	THE ROYAL MOUNTED PATROL	COL	1941	CHARLES STARRETT
___	ROLLING DOWN THE GREAT DIVIDE	PRC	1942	BOYD/DAVIS/POWELL
___	LAW AND ORDER	PRC	1942	BUSTER CRABBE
___	TEXAS JUSTICE	PRC	1942	GEORGE HOUSTON
___	DEERSLAYER	REP	1943	BRUCE KELLOGG
___	RAIDERS OF GHOST CITY	UNI	1944	DENNIS MOORE

HELEN McKELLER

	Title	Studio	Year	Star
___	THE GREAT TRAIN ROBBERY	REP	1941	BOB STEELE
___	GANGS OF SONORA	REP	1941	LIVINGSTON/STEELE
___	DOWN MEXICO WAY	REP	1941	GENE AUTRY
___	SUNDOWN KID	REP	1942	DON BARRY

EVA McKENZIE

	Title	Studio	Year	Star
___	LIGHTNING BILL	SUP	1934	BUFFALO BILL, JR.
___	PIONEER TRAIL	COL	1938	JACK LUDEN
___	WELLS FARGO DAYS	WB	1944	DENNIS MOORE

FAY McKENZIE

	Title	Studio	Year	Star
___	BOSS COWBOY	SUP	1934	BUDDY ROOSEVELT
___	THE SUNDOWN TRAIL	IMP	1934	WALLY WALES
___	DEATH RIDES THE RANGE	COL	1940	KEN MAYNARD
___	DOWN MEXICO WAY	REP	1941	GENE AUTRY
___	SIERRA SUE	REP	1941	GENE AUTRY
___	COWBOY SERENADE	REP	1942	GENE AUTRY
___	HEART OF THE RIO GRANDE	REP	1942	GENE AUTRY
___	HOME IN WYOMING	REP	1942	GENE AUTRY
___	THE SINGING SHERIFF	UNI	1944	BOB CROSBY

MYRA McKINNEY (MIRA)

	Title	Studio	Year	Star
___	BLAZING SIXES	WB	1937	DICK FORAN
___	BADMAN FROM RED BUTTE	UNI	1940	JOHNNY MACK BROWN
___	ROUGH RIDERS OF CHEYENNE	REP	1945	SUNSET CARSON
___	TRAIL TO LAREDO	COL	1948	CHARLES STARRETT
___	TRAIL OF THE RUSTLERS	COL	1950	CHARLES STARRETT

___HEART OF THE ROCKIES...............REP .....1951.....ROY ROGERS

MARY MacLAREN

___WESTWARD HO...............................REP .....1935.....JOHN WAYNE
___THE NEW FRONTIER.......................REP .....1935.....JOHN WAYNE
___SADDLE ACES.................................RES .....1935.....REX BELL
___KING OF THE PECOS.......................REP .....1936.....JOHN WAYNE
___RECKLESS RANGER.........................COL .....1937.....BOB ALLEN
___THE FARGO KID..............................RKO .....1940.....TIM HOLT
___PRAIRIE PIONEERS.........................REP .....1941.....BOB LIVINGSTON
___FIGHTING VALLEY...........................PRC .....1943.....NEWILL/O'BRIEN
___SIX GUN GOSPEL.............................MON ....1943.....JOHNNY MACK BROWN
___THE NAVAJO TRAIL..........................MON ....1945.....JOHNNY MACK BROWN
___FRONTIER FEUD..............................MON ....1945.....JOHNNY MACK BROWN
___CROSSED TRAILS.............................MON ....1948.....JOHNNY MACK BROWN

CATHERINE McLEOD

___THEY SHALL HAVE FAITH..............MON ....1945.....JOHNNY MACK BROWN
___THE FABULOUS TEXAN..................REP .....1947.....BILL ELLIOTT
___OLD LOS ANGELES.........................REP .....1948.....BILL ELLIOTT

BLANCHE MEHAFFEY

___SUNRISE TRAIL...............................TIF ....1931.....BOB STEELE
___RIDERS OF THE NORTH.................SYN .....1931.....BOB CUSTER
___DUGAN OF THE BADLANDS..........MON ....1931.....BILL CODY
___MOUNTED FURY.............................WW ......1931.....JOHN BOWERS
___BORDER GUNS...............................AYW ....1934.....BILL CODY
___THE OUTLAW TAMER......................EMP .....1934.....LANE CHANDLER
___THE COWBOY AND THE BANDIT ..SUP .....1935.....REX LEASE
___NORTH OF ARIZONA.......................REL......1935.....JACK PERRIN
___THE SILENT CODE..........................S&S .....1935.....KANE RICHMOND
___WILDCAT SAUNDERS.......................ATL ......1936.....JACK PERRIN

TINA MENARD

___THE CACTUS KID.............................REL......1934.....JACK PERRIN
___LOSERS END...................................REL......1934.....JACK PERRIN
___CHEYENNE TORNADO....................KEN .....1935.....REB RUSSELL
___THE TRAITOR..................................PUR .....1936.....TIM McCOY

IRIS MEREDITH

___COWBOY STAR................................COL .....1936.....CHARLES STARRETT
___RIO GRANDE RANGER....................COL .....1936.....BOB ALLEN
___THE GAMBLING TERROR................REP .....1937.....JOHNNY MACK BROWN
___TRAIL OF VENGEANCE...................REP .....1937.....JOHNNY MACK BROWN
___A LAWMAN IS BORN........................REP .....1937.....JOHNNY MACK BROWN

___THE MYSTERY OF THE HOODED HORSEMAN .GN .... 1937 ..... TEX RITTER
___OUTLAWS OF THE PRAIRIE .... COL ..... 1937 ..... CHARLES STARRETT
___CATTLE RAIDERS .... COL ..... 1938 ..... CHARLES STARRETT
___CALL OF THE ROCKIES .... COL ..... 1938 ..... CHARLES STARRETT
___LAW OF THE PLAINS .... COL ..... 1938 ..... CHARLES STARRETT
___WEST OF CHEYENNE .... COL ..... 1938 ..... CHARLES STARRETT
___SOUTH OF ARIZONA .... COL ..... 1938 ..... CHARLES STARRETT
___THE COLORADO TRAIL .... COL ..... 1938 ..... CHARLES STARRETT
___WEST OF THE SANTA FE .... COL ..... 1938 ..... CHARLES STARRETT
___THE THUNDERING WEST .... COL ..... 1939 ..... CHARLES STARRETT
___TEXAS STAMPEDE .... COL ..... 1939 ..... CHARLES STARRETT
___SPOILERS OF THE RANGE .... COL ..... 1939 ..... CHARLES STARRETT
___WESTERN CARAVANS .... COL ..... 1939 ..... CHARLES STARRETT
___THE MAN FROM SUNDOWN .... COL ..... 1939 ..... CHARLES STARRETT
___RIDERS OF BLACK RIVER .... COL ..... 1939 ..... CHARLES STARRETT
___OUTPOST OF THE MOUNTIES ...... COL ..... 1939 ..... CHARLES STARRETT
___TAMING OF THE WEST .... COL ..... 1939 ..... BILL ELLIOTT
___TWO FISTED RANGERS .... COL ..... 1940 ..... CHARLES STARRETT
___BLAZING SIX SHOOTERS .... COL ..... 1940 ..... CHARLES STARRETT
___THE MAN FROM TUMBLEWEEDS .COL ..... 1940 ..... BILL ELLIOTT
___TEXAS STAGECOACH .... COL ..... 1940 ..... CHARLES STARRETT
___THE RETURN OF WILD BILL .... COL ..... 1940 ..... BILL ELLIOTT
___THUNDERING FRONTIER .... COL ..... 1940 ..... CHARLES STARRETT
___SON OF DAVY CROCKETT .... COL ..... 1941 ..... BILL ELLIOTT
___THE RANGERS TAKE OVER .... PRC ..... 1942 ..... NEWILL/O'BRIEN
___THE KID RIDES AGAIN .... PRC ..... 1943 ..... BUSTER CRABBE

LYNN MERRICK

___RAGTIME COWBOY JOE .... UNI ...... 1940 ..... JOHNNY MACK BROWN
___TWO GUN SHERIFF .... REP ..... 1941 ..... DON BARRY
___DESERT BANDIT .... REP ..... 1941 ..... DON BARRY
___KANSAS CYCLONE .... REP ..... 1941 ..... DON BARRY
___THE APACHE KID .... REP ..... 1941 ..... DON BARRY
___DEATH VALLEY OUTLAWS .... REP ..... 1941 ..... DON BARRY
___A MISSOURI OUTLAW .... REP ..... 1941 ..... DON BARRY
___ARIZONA TERROR .... REP ..... 1942 ..... DON BARRY
___STAGECOACH EXPRESS .... REP ..... 1942 ..... DON BARRY
___JESSE JAMES, JR. .... REP ..... 1942 ..... DON BARRY
___CYCLONE KID .... REP ..... 1942 ..... DON BARRY
___THE SOMBRERO KID .... REP ..... 1942 ..... DON BARRY
___OUTLAWS OF PINE RIDGE .... REP ..... 1942 ..... DON BARRY
___DEAD MANS' GULCH .... REP ..... 1943 ..... DON BARRY
___CARSON CITY CYCLONE .... REP ..... 1943 ..... DON BARRY
___DAYS OF OLD CHEYENNE .... REP ..... 1943 ..... DON BARRY

___FUGITIVE FROM SONORA ....REP .....1943.....DON BARRY

GERTRUDE MESSINGER

___RIDERS OF THE DESERT..............WW ......1932.....BOB STEELE
___HIDDEN VALLEY ....MON ....1932.....BOB STEELE
___LAWLESS VALLEY ....KEN .....1932.....LANE CHANDLER
___WAGON TRAIL...............................AJA ......1935.....HARRY CAREY
___RUSTLERS' PARADISE ....AJA ......1935.....HARRY CAREY
___MELODY TRAIL ....REP .....1935.....GENE AUTRY
___THE RIDER OF THE LAW...............SUP .....1935.....BOB STEELE
___ACES WILD ....COM ....1935.....HARRY CAREY
___BLAZING JUSTICE ....SPE .....1936.....BILL CODY
___FEUD OF THE RANGE ....MET .....1939.....BOB STEELE

BETTY MILES

___THE RETURN OF DANIEL BOONE COL .....1941.....BILL ELLIOTT
___WANDERERS OF THE WEST ....MON ....1941.....TOM KEENE
___THE DRIFTING KID ....MON ....1941.....TOM KEENE
___RIDING THE SUNSET TRAIL ....MON ....1941.....TEX RITTER
___RIDING THE CHEROKEE TRAIL ....MON ....1941.....TEX RITTER
___LONE STAR LAW MEN ....MON ....1941.....TOM KEENE
___WILD HORSE STAMPEDE..............MON ....1943.....MAYNARD/GIBSON
___THE LAW RIDES AGAIN ....MON ....1943.....TRAILBLAZERS
___LAW OF THE SADDLE ....PRC .....1943.....BOB LIVINGSTON
___WESTWARD BOUND ....MON ....1944.....TRAILBLAZERS
___SONORA STAGECOACH ....MON ....1944.....GIBSON/STEELE
___GANGSTERS OF THE FRONTIER..PRC .....1944.....RITTER/O'BRIEN

LORRAINE MILLER

___RIDERS OF THE RIO GRANDE ......REP .....1943.....STEELE/TYLER
___BEYOND THE LAST FRONTIER .....REP .....1943.....EDDIE DEW
___THREE IN THE SADDLE..................PRC .....1945.....RITTER/O'BRIEN
___FRONTIER FUGITIVES....................PRC .....1945.....RISSER/O'BRIEN
___BORDER BADMEN ....PRC .....1945.....BUSTER CRABBE
___LONESOME TRAIL ....MON ....1945.....JIMMY WAKELY
___AMBUSH TRAIL ....PRC .....1946.....BOB STEELE

GENEVA MITCHELL

___FIGHTING SHADOWS......................COL .....1935.....TIM McCOY
___WESTERN COURAGE ....COL .....1935.....KEN MAYNARD
___LAWLESS RIDERS ....COL .....1935.....KEN MAYNARD
___THE CATTLE THIEF ....COL .....1936.....KEN MAYNARD

RUTH MIX

___RED FORK RANGE ....B4 ....1931.....WALLY WALES

___FIGHTING PIONEERS ....RES .....1935.....REX BELL
___GUN FIRE ....RES .....1935.....REX BELL
___SADDLE ACES.................................RES .....1935.....REX BELL
___THE TONTO KID ....RES .....1935.....REX BELL
___RIDING AVENGER ....DIV.......1936.....HOOT GIBSON

CONSTANCE MOORE

___BORDER WOLVES...........................UNI ......1938.....BOB BAKER
___THE LAST STAND ....UNI ......1938.....BOB BAKER
___IN OLD SACRAMENTO ....REP .....1946.....BILL ELLIOTT

PAULINE MOORE

___WAGON WHEELS ....PAR .....1934.....RANDOLPH SCOTT
___DAYS OF JESSE JAMES ....REP .....1939.....ROY ROGERS
___YOUNG BUFFALO BILL ....REP .....1940.....ROY ROGERS
___THE CARSON CITY KID ....REP .....1940.....ROY ROGERS
___COLORADO ....REP .....1940.....ROY ROGERS
___THE TRAIL BLAZERS ....REP .....1940.....LIVINGSTON/STEELE
___ARKANSAS JUDGE..........................REP .....1941.....ROY ROGERS

PATSY MORAN

___THE COWBOY FROM SUNDOWN..MON ....1940.....TEX RITTER
___THE GOLDEN TRAIL........................MON ....1940.....TEX RITTER
___SONG OF THE DRIFTER ....MON ....1948.....JIMMY WAKELY

PEGGY MORAN

___RHYTHM OF THE SADDLE ....REP .....1938.....GENE AUTRY
___WEST OF CARSON CITY ....UNI ......1940.....JOHNNY MACK BROWN
___KING OF THE COWBOYS ....REP .....1943.....ROY ROGERS

KAY MORLEY

___SIX GUN SERENADE........................MON ....1947.....JIMMY WAKELY
___CODE OF THE SADDLE ....MON ....1947.....JOHNNY MACK BROWN
___OUTLAW BRAND.............................MON ....1948.....JIMMY WAKELY
___TRAILS END....................................MON ....1949.....JOHNNY MACK BROWN

FRANCES MORRIS (WRIGHT)

___THE RIDIN' FOOL.............................TIF ....1931.....BOB STEELE
___NEVADA CYCLONE ....REL......1934.....FRED HUMES
___BOSS COWBOY ....SPR .....1934.....BUDDY ROOSEVELT
___THE RAWHIDE TERROR.................SEC .....1934.....ART MIX
___PALS OF THE RANGE ....SPR .....1935.....REX LEASE
___THE BIG SHOW ....REP .....1936.....GENE AUTRY
___LUMBERJACK ....UA ....1944.....WILLIAM BOYD

MOVITA

___ROSE OF THE RIO GRANDE .... MON .... 1938 ..... JOHN CARROLL
___WOLF CALL .... MON .... 1939 ..... JOHN CARROLL
___THE MYSTERIOUS DESPERADO .. RKO ..... 1949 ..... TIM HOLT
___WILD HORSE AMBUSH .... REP ..... 1952 ..... MICHAEL CHAPIN

HELEN MOWERY

___THE FIGHTING FRONTIERSMAN ... COL ..... 1946 ..... CHARLES STARRETT
___RANGE BEYOND THE BLUE .... PRC ..... 1947 ..... EDDIE DEAN
___ACROSS THE BADLANDS .... COL ..... 1950 ..... CHARLES STARRETT
___THE KID FROM BROKEN GUN .... COL ..... 1952 ..... CHARLES STARRETT

ESTHER MUIR

___THE LAW WEST OF TOMBSTONE RKO ..... 1938 ..... HARRY CAREY
___WESTERN JAMBOREE .... REP ..... 1938 ..... GENE AUTRY
___THE GIRL AND THE GAMBLER ...... RKO ..... 1939 ..... LEO CARRILLO

ANNE NAGEL

___GUNS OF THE PECOS .... FN .... 1937 ..... DICK FORAN
___THE DEVILS' SADDLE LEGION ...... WB .... 1937 ..... DICK FORAN
___ROAD AGENT .... UNI .... 1941 ..... DICK FORAN
___STAGECOACH BUCKAROO .... UNI .... 1942 ..... JOHNNY MACK BROWN

NOREEN NASH

___THE RED STALLION .... EL .... 1947 ..... ROBERT PAIGE
___STORM OVER WYOMING .... RKO ..... 1950 ..... TIM HOLT
___ROAD AGENT .... RKO ..... 1952 ..... TIM HOLT
___THE LONE RANGER AND THE .... UA .... 1958 ..... CLAYTON MOORE
LOST CITY OF GOLD

NOEL NEILL

___OVER THE SANTA FE TRAIL .... COL ..... 1947 ..... KEN CURTIS
___GUN RUNNER .... MON .... 1949 ..... JIMMY WAKELY
___SON OF A BADMAN .... SG .... 1949 ..... LASH LARUE
___ABILENE TRAIL .... MON .... 1951 ..... WHIP WILSON
___WHISTLING HILLS .... MON .... 1951 ..... JOHNNY MACK BROWN
___MONTANA INCIDENT .... MON .... 1952 ..... WHIP WILSON
___THE LAWLESS RIDER .... UA .... 1954 ..... JOHNNY CARPENTER

MARY NEWTON

___THE LONE HAND TEXAN .... COL ..... 1947 ..... CHARLES STARRETT
___THE LAST DAYS OF BOOT HILL .... COL ..... 1947 ..... CHARLES STARRETT
___THE MARAUDERS .... UA .... 1947 ..... WILLIAM BOYD
___BADMEN OF TOMBSTONE .... AA .... 1949 ..... BARRY NELSON

Noel Neill with Rand Brooks

___THE DESERT VIGILANTE .... COL ..... 1949 ..... CHARLES STARRETT
___JUNCTION CITY .... COL ..... 1952 ..... CHARLES STARRETT

JANE NIGH

___FIGHTING MAN OF THE PLAINS ... FOX ..... 1949 ..... RANDOLPH SCOTT
___BORDER TREASURE .... RKO ..... 1950 ..... TIM HOLT
___RIO GRANDE PATROL .... RKO ..... 1950 ..... TIM HOLT
___FORT OSAGE .... MON .... 1952 ..... ROD CAMERON
___RODEO .... MON .... 1952 ..... JOHN ARCHER

EVA NOVAK

___PHANTOM OF THE DESERT .... SYN ..... 1930 ..... JACK PERRIN
___THE TOPEKA TERROR .... REP ..... 1945 ..... ALLAN LANE
___ROBIN HOOD OF TEXAS .... REP ..... 1947 ..... GENE AUTRY
___HELLFIRE .... REP ..... 1949 ..... BILL ELLIOTT

MOLLY O'DAY

___LAW OF THE 45'S .... FD .... 1935 ..... GUINN WILLIAMS
___LAWLESS BORDERS .... SPE ..... 1935 ..... BILL CODY

___SKULL AND CROWN .... REL...... 1935..... RIN TIN TIN

NELL O'DAY

___SMOKE LIGHTNING .... FOX ..... 1933..... GEORGE O'BRIEN
___SON OF ROARING DAN .... UNI....... 1940..... JOHNNY MACK BROWN
___RAGTIME COWBOY JOE .... UNI....... 1940..... JOHNNY MACK BROWN
___LAW AND ORDER .... UNI....... 1940..... JOHNNY MACK BROWN
___PONY POST .... UNI....... 1940..... JOHNNY MACK BROWN
___BOSS OF BULLION CITY .... UNI....... 1941..... JOHNNY MACK BROWN
___BURY ME NOT ON THE LONE .... UNI....... 1941..... JOHNNY MACK BROWN
PRAIRIE
___LAW OF THE RANGE .... UNI....... 1941..... JOHNNY MACK BROWN
___RAWHIDE RANGERS .... UNI....... 1941..... JOHNNY MACK BROWN
___THE MAN FROM MONTANA .... UNI....... 1941..... JOHNNY MACK BROWN
___THE MASKED RIDER .... UNI....... 1941..... JOHNNY MACK BROWN
___ARIZONA CYCLONE .... UNI....... 1941..... JOHNNY MACK BROWN
___FIGHTING BILL FARGO .... UNI....... 1941..... JOHNNY MACK BROWN
___STAGECOACH BUCKAROO .... UNI....... 1942..... JOHNNY MACK BROWN
___ARIZONA STAGECOACH .... MON ..... 1942..... CORRIGAN/KING
___PIRATES OF THE PRAIRIE .... RKO ..... 1942..... TIM HOLT
___THUNDERING TRAILS .... REP ..... 1943..... TYLER/STEELE
___RETURN OF THE RANGERS .... PRC ..... 1943..... NEWILL/O'BRIEN
___BOSS OF RAWHIDE .... PRC ..... 1943..... NEWILL/O'BRIEN

GEORGIA O'DELL

___BIG CALIBRE .... SUP ..... 1935..... BOB STEELE
___WEST OF NEVADA .... COL ..... 1936..... REX BELL
___THE SINGING OUTLAW .... UNI....... 1938..... BOB BAKER
___GUILTY TRAIL .... UNI....... 1938..... BOB BAKER

MARTHA O'DRISCOLL

___WAGON TRAIN .... RKO ..... 1940..... TIM HOLT
___UNDER WESTERN SKIES .... UNI....... 1945..... NOAH BEERY, JR.
___THE DALTONS RIDE AGAIN .... UNI....... 1945..... ALAN CURTIS

DOROTHY PAGE

___WATER RUSTLERS .... GN .... 1939..... DAVE O'BRIEN
___RIDE 'EM COWGIRL .... GN .... 1939..... MILTON FROME
___THE SINGING COWGIRL .... GN .... 1939..... DAVE O'BRIEN

SARAH PADDEN

___FORBIDDEN VALLEY .... UNI....... 1938..... NOAH BEERY, JR.
___LONE STAR RAIDERS .... REP ..... 1940..... LIVINGSTON/STEELE
___IN OLD COLORADO .... PAR ..... 1941..... WILLIAM BOYD
___SUNSET IN WYOMING .... REP ..... 1941..... GENE AUTRY

___OUTLAWS OF THE CHEROKEE.....REP .....1941.....STEELE/TYLER
TRAIL
___HEART OF THE RIO GRANDE........REP .....1942.....GENE AUTRY
___THE DEVILS' TRAIL ....COL .....1942.....ELLIOTT/RITTER
___LAW AND ORDER ....PRC .....1942.....BUSTER CRABBE
___RIDERS OF THE WEST ....MON ....1942.....JONES/McCOY
___RANGE LAW ....MON ....1944.....JOHNNY MACK BROWN
___TRAIL TO GUNSIGHT ....UNI ......1944.....EDDIE DEW
___GHOST GUNS..................................MON ....1944.....JOHNNY MACK BROWN
___WILDFIRE..SCR .....1945.....BOB STEELE
___RIDERS OF THE DAWN ....MON ....1945.....JIMMY WAKELY
___MARSHAL OF LAREDO ....REP .....1945.....BILL ELLIOTT
___SONG OF OLD WYOMING ....PRC .....1945.....EDDIE DEAN
___WILD WEST ....PRC .....1946.....EDDIE DEAN
___TRAIL STREET ....RKO .....1947.....RANDOLPH SCOTT
___RANGE JUSTICE.............................MON ....1948.....JOHNNY MACK BROWN
___FRONTIER REVENGE ....SG ....1948.....LASH LARUE
___GUNSLINGERS ....MON ....1950.....WHIP WILSON
___THE MISSOURIANS ....REP .....1950.....MONTE HALE
___UTAH WAGON TRAIN.......................REP .....1951.....REX ALLEN

CECILIA PARKER

___THE RAINBOW TRAIL.......................FOX .....1932.....GEORGE O'BRIEN
___THE GAY CABALLERO ....FOX .....1932.....GEORGE O'BRIEN
___MYSTERY RANCH ....FOX .....1932.....GEORGE O'BRIEN
___TOMBSTONE CANYON ....WW ......1932.....KEN MAYNARD
___UNKNOWN VALLEY..........................COL .....1933.....BUCK JONES
___RAINBOW RANCH............................MON ....1933.....REX BELL
___THE FUGITIVE.................................MON ....1933.....REX BELL
___THE TRAIL DRIVE ....UNI ......1933.....KEN MAYNARD
___RIDERS OF DESTINY ....MON ....1933.....JOHN WAYNE
___GUN JUSTICE..................................UNI ......1933.....KEN MAYNARD
___THE MAN TRAILER ....COL .....1934.....BUCK JONES
___HONOR OF THE RANGE ....UNI ......1934.....KEN MAYNARD
___THE MINE WITH THE IRON DOOR COL .....1936.....RICHARD ARLEN
___HOLLYWOOD COWBOY..................RKO .....1937.....GEORGE O'BRIEN
___ROLL ALONG COWBOY ....20T ......1937.....SMITH BALLEW

JEAN PARKER

___KNIGHTS OF THE RANGE ....PAR .....1940.....RUSSELL HAYDEN
___THE GIRL FROM ALASKA ....REP .....1942.....RAY MIDDLETON
___DEERSLAYER ....REP .....1943.....BRUCE KELLOGG

HELEN PARRISH

___SUNSET SERENADE ....REP .....1942.....ROY ROGERS

___QUICK ON THE TRIGGER .... COL ..... 1948 ..... CHARLES STARRETT
___THE WOLF HUNTERS .... MON .... 1949 ..... KIRBY GRANT

DOROTHY PATRICK

___REDWOOD FOREST TRAIL .... REP ..... 1950 ..... REX ALLEN
___UNDER MEXICALI STARS .... REP ..... 1950 ..... REX ALLEN
___DESERT PASSAGE .... RKO ..... 1952 ..... TIM HOLT
___ROAD AGENT .... RKO ..... 1952 ..... TIM HOLT
___SAVAGE FRONTIER .... REP ..... 1953 ..... ALLAN LANE
___THE OUTLAW STALLION .... COL ..... 1954 ..... PHIL CAREY

GAIL PATRICK

___THE MYSTERIOUS RIDER .... PAR ..... 1933 ..... KENT TAYLOR
___TO THE LAST MAN .... PAR ..... 1933 ..... RANDOLPH SCOTT
___WAGON WHEELS .... PAR ..... 1934 ..... RANDOLPH SCOTT
___WANDERER OF THE WASTELAND PAR ..... 1935 ..... DEAN JAGGER
___CHEYENNE ROUNDUP .... UNI .... 1943 ..... BROWN/RITTER
___THE PLAINSMAN AND THE LADY . REP ..... 1946 ..... BILL ELLIOTT
___KING OF THE WILD HORSES .... COL ..... 1947 ..... PRESTON FOSTER

SHIRLEY PATTERSON

___NORTH OF THE ROCKIES .... COL ..... 1942 ..... ELLIOTT/RITTER
___RIDERS OF THE NORTHLAND .... COL ..... 1942 ..... CHARLES STARRETT
___RIDING THROUGH NEVADA .... COL ..... 1942 ..... CHARLES STARRETT
___LAW OF THE NORTHWEST .... COL ..... 1943 ..... CHARLES STARRETT

Shirley Patterson with Eddie Dean

___THE TEXAS KID .... MON .... 1943 ..... JOHNNY MACK BROWN
___THE VIGILANTES RIDE .... COL ..... 1944 ..... RUSSELL HAYDEN
___RIDING WEST .... COL ..... 1944 ..... CHARLES STARRETT
___DRIFTING RIVER .... PRC ..... 1946 ..... EDDIE DEAN
___TUMBLEWEED TRAIL .... PRC ..... 1946 ..... EDDIE DEAN
___STARS OVER TEXAS .... PRC ..... 1946 ..... EDDIE DEAN
___BLACK HILLS .... EL .... 1947 ..... EDDIE DEAN

SALLY PAYNE

___THE BIG SHOW .... REP ..... 1936 ..... GENE AUTRY
___MAN FROM MUSIC MOUNTAIN ..... REP ..... 1938 ..... GENE AUTRY
___YOUNG BILL HICKOK .... REP ..... 1940 ..... ROY ROGERS
___ROBIN HOOD OF THE PECOS .... REP ..... 1941 ..... ROY ROGERS
___IN OLD CHEYENNE .... REP ..... 1941 ..... ROY ROGERS
___SHERIFF OF TOMBSTONE .... REP ..... 1941 ..... ROY ROGERS
___NEVADA CITY .... REP ..... 1941 ..... ROY ROGERS
___BAD MAN OF DEADWOOD .... REP ..... 1941 ..... ROY ROGERS
___JESSE JAMES AT BAY .... REP ..... 1941 ..... ROY ROGERS
___RED RIVER VALLEY .... REP ..... 1941 ..... ROY ROGERS
___MAN FROM CHEYENNE .... REP ..... 1942 ..... ROY ROGERS
___ROMANCE ON THE RANGE .... REP ..... 1942 ..... ROY ROGERS

BARBARA PEPPER

___THE SAGEBRUSH TROUBADOR ... REP ..... 1935 ..... GENE AUTRY
___THE SINGING VAGABOND .... REP ..... 1935 ..... GENE AUTRY
___COLORADO SUNSET .... REP ..... 1939 ..... GENE AUTRY
___TERROR TRAIL .... COL ..... 1946 ..... CHARLES STARRETT

JOAN PERRY

___THE GALLANT DEFENDER .... COL ..... 1935 ..... CHARLES STARRETT
___HEIR TO TROUBLE .... COL ..... 1935 ..... KEN MAYNARD
___THE MYSTERIOUS AVENGER .... COL ..... 1936 ..... CHARLES STARRETT

ROSE PLUMMER

___LAW OF THE WEST .... WW ...... 1932 ..... BOB STEELE
___THE PECOS KID .... COM .... 1935 ..... FRED KOHLER, JR.
___GIT ALONG LITTLE DOGIES .... REP ..... 1937 ..... GENE AUTRY
___ROVING TUMBLEWEEDS .... REP ..... 1939 ..... GENE AUTRY
___TAKE ME BACK TO OKLAHOMA .... MON .... 1940 ..... TEX RITTER
___CYCLONE KID .... REP ..... 1942 ..... DON BARRY
___CATTLE STAMPEDE .... PRC ..... 1943 ..... BUSTER CRABBE
___TRAIL OF TERROR .... PRC ..... 1943 ..... NEWILL/O'BRIEN
___BORDERTOWN GUNFIGHTERS .... REP ..... 1943 ..... BILL ELLIOTT
___BULLETS AND SADDLES .... MON .... 1943 ..... CORRIGAN/MOORE
___PHANTOM OF THE PLAINS .... REP ..... 1945 ..... BILL ELLIOTT

JEAN PORTER

___HEART OF THE RIO GRANDE........REP .....1942.....GENE AUTRY
___HOME IN WYOMING........................REP .....1942.....GENE AUTRY
___CALABOOSE...................................UA........1943.....JIMMY ROGERS
___SAN FERNANDO VALLEY...............REP .....1944.....ROY ROGERS

MAUDIE PRICKETT

___GOLD MINE IN THE SKY.................REP .....1938.....GENE AUTRY
___TWO FISTED STRANGER...............COL .....1946.....CHARLES STARRETT
___THE FIGHTING FRONTIERSMAN...COL .....1946.....CHARLES STARRETT
___THE LONE HAND TEXAN................COL .....1947.....CHARLES STARRETT
___SONG OF IDAHO.............................COL .....1948.....KIRBY GRANT
___THE COWBOY AND THE INDIANS.COL .....1949.....GENE AUTRY
___BEYOND THE PURPLE HILLS........COL .....1950.....GENE AUTRY
___PECOS RIVER................................COL .....1951.....CHARLES STARRETT

EVA PUIG

___BELOW THE BORDER.....................MON ....1942.....JONES/McCOY
___VENGEANCE OF THE WEST..........COL .....1942.....ELLIOTT/RITTER
___UNDERCOVER MAN........................UA........1942.....WILLIAM BOYD
___THE CISCO KID RETURNS............MON ....1945.....DUNCAN RENALDO
___THE PLAINSMAN AND THE LADY .REP .....1946.....BILL ELLIOTT
___WILD BEAUTY................................UNI.......1946.....DON PORTER

NANA QUARTERO

___ARIZONA TERRORS........................TIF ....1933.....KEN MAYNARD
___THE MAN FROM MONTERREY......WB ....1933.....JOHN WAYNE
___THE CYCLONE RANGER................SPE .....1935.....BILL CODY
___LEFT HANDED LAW........................UNI.......1937.....BUCK JONES

MARIE QUILLAN

___THE HURRICANE HORSEMAN.......KENT ...1931.....LANE CHANDLER
___THE CHEYENNE CYCLONE...........KENT ...1932.....LANE CHANDLER
___SADDLE BUSTER............................RKO.....1932.....TOM KEENE
___MELODY TRAIL..............................REP .....1935.....GENE AUTRY
___THE SINGING VAGABOND.............REP .....1935.....GENE AUTRY

ELLA RAINES

___TALL IN THE SADDLE.....................RKO.....1944.....JOHN WAYNE
___THE WALKING HILLS......................RKO.....1949.....RANDOLPH SCOTT
___SINGING GUNS..............................REP .....1950.....VAUGHAN MONROE

ISABEL RANDOLPH

___RIDE TENDERFOOT, RIDE.............REP .....1940.....GENE AUTRY
___THUNDERING CARAVANS.............REP .....1952.....ALLAN LANE

___BORDER CITY RUSTLERS ....AA .... 1953..... GUY MADISON

LOIS RANSOM

___UNDER TEXAS SKIES ....REP ..... 1940..... 3 MESQUITEERS
___PIERRE OF THE PLAINS..................MGM .... 1942..... JOHN CARROLL
___THE RENEGADE ....PRC ..... 1943..... BUSTER CRABBE

FELICE RAYMOND

___TRAIL OF THE MOUNTIES..............SG .... 1947..... RUSSELL HAYDEN
___FIGHTING MUSTANG ....AST...... 1948..... SUNSET CARSON
___LOADED PISTOLS ....COL ..... 1948..... GENE AUTRY
___COWTOWN ....COL ..... 1950..... GENE AUTRY

JANE REGAN

___WEST ON PARADE ....REL...... 1934..... DENNY MEADOWS
___THE CACTUS KID ....REL...... 1934..... JACK PERRIN
___SILVER BULLET ....REL...... 1935..... TOM TYLER
___RIDIN' THRU ....REL...... 1935..... TOM TYLER
___TEXAS JACK......................................REL...... 1935..... JACK PERRIN

DOROTHY REVIER

___THE BAD MAN ....FN .... 1930..... WALTER HUSTON
___THE AVENGER..................................COL ..... 1931..... BUCK JONES
___ARM OF THE LAW ....MON .... 1932..... REX BELL
___THRILL HUNTER ....COL ..... 1933..... BUCK JONES
___THE FIGHTING RANGER ....COL ..... 1934..... BUCK JONES
___WHEN A MAN SEES RED ....UNI ...... 1934..... BUCK JONES
___THE EAGLES' BROOD.......................PAR ..... 1935..... WILLIAM BOYD
___THE COWBOY AND THE KID ....UNI ...... 1936..... BUCK JONES

MARJORIE REYNOLDS

___TEX RIDES WITH THE BOY SCOUTS GN .... 1938..... TEX RITTER
___OVERLAND EXPRESS ....COL ..... 1938..... BUCK JONES
___SIX SHOOTING SHERIFF................GN .... 1938..... KEN MAYNARD
___WESTERN TRAILS ....UNI ...... 1938..... BOB BAKER
___MANS' COUNTRY.............................MON .... 1938..... JACK RANDALL
___THE BLACK BANDIT ....UNI ...... 1938..... BOB BAKER
___GUILTY TRAIL ....UNI ...... 1938..... BOB BAKER
___THE PHANTOM STAGE ....UNI ...... 1939..... BOB BAKER
___RACKETEERS OF THE RANGE .....RKO ..... 1939..... GEORGE O'BRIEN
___TIMBER STAMPEDE ....RKO ..... 1939..... GEORGE O'BRIEN
___ROBIN HOOD OF THE PECOS ....REP ..... 1941..... ROY ROGERS
___CYCLONE ON HORSEBACK...........RKO ..... 1941..... TIM HOLT
___DUDE COWBOY ....RKO ..... 1941..... TIM HOLT
___BADMEN OF TOMBSTONE ....AA .... 1949..... BARRY SULLIVAN

Marjorie Reynolds with Carlyle Moore

ELAINE RILEY

___DEVIL'S PLAYGROUND ....UA........1946.....WILLIAM BOYD
___DANGEROUS VENTURE ....UA........1947.....WILLIAM BOYD
___SINISTER JOURNEY.......................UA........1948.....WILLIAM BOYD
___BORROWED TROUBLE ....UA........1948.....WILLIAM BOYD
___FALSE PARADISE ....UA........1948.....WILLIAM BOYD
___STRANGE GAMBLE ....UA........1948.....WILLIAM BOYD
___TRAILIN' WEST..............................WB ....1949.....CHILL WILLS
___RIDER FROM TUCSON ....RKO .....1950.....TIM HOLT
___HILLS OF UTAH ....COL .....1951.....GENE AUTRY
___LEADVILLE GUNSLINGER ....REP .....1952.....ALLAN LANE
___TEXAS BADMAN ....AA ....1953.....WAYNE MORRIS

ELIZABETH RISDON

___TALL IN THE SADDLE ....RKO .....1944.....JOHN WAYNE
___ROLL ON TEXAS MOON ....REP .....1946.....ROY ROGERS
___DOWN DAKOTA WAY ....REP .....1949.....ROY ROGERS
___HILLS OF OKLAHOMA ....REP .....1949.....REX ALLEN
___SIERRA...UNI.......1950.....AUDIE MURPHY
___IN OLD AMARILLO ....REP .....1951.....ROY ROGERS

BETTY ROADMAN

___BILLY THE KID RETURNS...............REP .....1938.....ROY ROGERS
___DOWN RIO GRANDE WAY..............COL .....1942.....CHARLES STARRETT
___RETURN OF THE DURANGO KID ..COL .....1945.....CHARLES STARRETT

ADELE ROBERTS

___ROARING RANGERS.......................COL .....1946.....CHARLES STARRETT
___THROW A SADDLE ON A STAR .....COL .....1946.....KEN CURTIS
___GALLOPING THUNDER...................COL .....1946.....CHARLES STARRETT
___DESERT HORSEMAN ....COL .....1946.....CHARLES STARRETT

LYNNE ROBERTS

___HEART OF THE ROCKIES ....REP .....1937.....LIVINGSTON/CORRIGAN
___CALL THE MESQUITEERS..............REP .....1938.....LIVINGSTON/CORRIGAN
___BILLY THE KID RETURNS...............REP .....1938.....ROY ROGERS
___COME ON RANGERS ....REP .....1938.....ROY ROGERS
___SHINE ON HARVEST MOON ....REP .....1938.....ROY ROGERS
___ROUGH RIDERS ROUNDUP ....REP .....1939.....ROY ROGERS
___FRONTIER PONY EXPRESS ....REP .....1939.....ROY ROGERS
___SOUTHWARD HO...........................REP .....1939.....ROY ROGERS
___IN OLD CALIENTE ....REP .....1939.....ROY ROGERS
___HI YO SILVER ....REP .....1940.....LEE POWELL
___ROMANCE OF THE RIO GRANDE .REP .....1941.....CESAR ROMERO
___RIDE ON VAQUERO ....REP .....1941.....CESAR ROMERO
___LAST OF THE DUANES ....20T ......1941.....GEORGE MONTGOMERY
___RIDERS OF THE PURPLE SAGE ...20T ......1941.....GEORGE MONTGOMERY
___THE BIG BONANZA..........................REP .....1944.....RICHARD ARLEN
___SIOUX CITY SUE.............................REP .....1946.....GENE AUTRY
___SADDLE PALS ....REP .....1947.....GENE AUTRY
___ROBIN HOOD OF TEXAS ....REP .....1947.....GENE AUTRY
___THE TIMBER TRAIL ....REP .....1948.....MONTE HALE
___EYES OF TEXAS ....REP .....1948.....ROY ROGERS
___SONS OF ADVENTURE ....REP .....1948.....RUSSELL HAYDEN
___THE BLAZING SUN ....COL .....1950.....GENE AUTRY
___DYNAMITE PASS ....RKO .....1950.....TIM HOLT
___CALL OF THE KLONDIKE ....MON ....1950.....KIRBY GRANT

FRANCES ROBINSON

___FORBIDDEN VALLEY ....UNI ......1938.....NOAH BERRY, JR.
___DESPERATE TRAILS........................UNI ......1939.....JOHNNY MACK BROWN
___RIDERS OF PASCO BASIN ....UNI ......1940.....JOHNNY MACK BROWN
___OUTLAWS OF THE PANHANDLE ...COL .....1941.....CHARLES STARRETT

RUTH ROBINSON

___ROLL ALONG COWBOY ....20T ......1937.....SMITH BALLEW

___THE KANSAS TERRORS .... REP ..... 1939 ..... LIVINGSTON/RENALDO
___COVERED WAGON DAYS .... REP ..... 1940 ..... LIVINGSTON/RENALDO
___TEXAS TERRORS .... REP ..... 1940 ..... DON BARRY
___ACROSS THE SIERRAS .... COL ..... 1941 ..... BILL ELLIOTT
___DOWN MEXICO WAY .... REP ..... 1941 ..... GENE AUTRY

CLAIRE ROCHELLE

___EMPTY SADDLES .... UNI .... 1936 ..... BUCK JONES
___GUNS IN THE DARK .... REP ..... 1937 ..... JOHNNY MACK BROWN
___BOOTHILL BRIGADE .... REP ..... 1937 ..... JOHNNY MACK BROWN
___RIDIN' THE LONE TRAIL .... REP ..... 1937 ..... BOB STEELE
___CODE OF THE FEARLESS .... SPE ..... 1939 ..... FRED SCOTT
___TWO GUN TROUBADOR .... SPE ..... 1939 ..... FRED SCOTT
___RIDERS OF THE SAGE .... MET ..... 1939 ..... BOB STEELE
___THE PAL FROM TEXAS .... MET ..... 1939 ..... BOB STEELE
___EL DIABLO RIDES .... MET ..... 1939 ..... BOB STEELE
___THE KID FROM SANTA FE .... MON .... 1940 ..... JACK RANDALL
___LIGHTNING STRIKES WEST .... COL ..... 1940 ..... KEN MAYNARD
___BUZZY RIDES THE RANGE .... ZI .... 1940 ..... BUZZY HENRY
___NORTH FROM THE LONE STAR .... COL ..... 1941 ..... BILL ELLIOTT
___TEXAS JUSTICE .... PRC ..... 1942 ..... GEORGE HOUSTON

ESTRALITA RODRIGUEZ (SEE ESTRALITA)

RUTH ROGERS

___SILVER ON THE SAGE .... PAR ..... 1939 ..... WILLIAM BOYD
___THE NIGHT RIDERS .... REP ..... 1939 ..... WAYNE/CORRIGAN
___MAN FROM TEXAS .... MON .... 1939 ..... TEX RITTER
___THE LIGHT OF THE WESTERN ...... PAR ..... 1940 ..... RUSSELL HAYDEN
STARS
___HIDDEN GOLD .... PAR ..... 1940 ..... WILLIAM BOYD

JEAN ROUVERAL

___BAR 20 RIDES AGAIN .... PAR ..... 1935 ..... WILLIAM BOYD
___THE LAW WEST OF TOMBSTONE RKO ..... 1938 ..... HARRY CAREY
___WESTERN JAMBOREE .... REP ..... 1938 ..... GENE AUTRY

MARY RUSSELL

___THE BIG SHOW .... REP ..... 1936 ..... GENE AUTRY
___ROARING LEAD .... REP ..... 1936 ..... LIVINGSTON/CORRIGAN
___RIDERS OF THE WHISTLING SKULL . REP ..... 1937 ..... LIVINGSTON/CORRIGAN
___THE SILVER TRAIL .... REL ...... 1937 ..... REX LEASE

ANN RUTHERFORD

___MELODY TRAIL .... REP ..... 1935 ..... GENE AUTRY

___THE SINGING VAGABOND ....REP .....1935.....GENE AUTRY
___THE OREGON TRAIL ....REP .....1936.....JOHN WAYNE
___THE LAWLESS NINETIES ....REP .....1936.....JOHN WAYNE
___COMING ROUND THE MOUNTAIN REP .....1936.....GENE AUTRY
___THE LONELY TRAIL.......................REP .....1936.....JOHN WAYNE
___PUBLIC COWBOY NO. 1 ....REP .....1937.....GENE AUTRY
___LARAMIE TRAIL ....REP .....1944.....BOB LIVINGSTON

SHEILAH RYAN

___THE GAY CABALLERO ....20T ......1940.....CESAR ROMERO
___LONE STAR RANGER......................20T ......1942.....JOHN KIMBROUGH
___SONG OF TEXAS ....REP .....1943.....ROY ROGERS
___THE COWBOY AND THE INDIANS.COL .....1949.....GENE AUTRY
___MULE TRAIN ....COL .....1950.....GENE AUTRY
___GOLD RAIDERS ....UA........1951.....GEORGE O'BRIEN
___WESTERN PACIFIC AGENT ....LIP ....1951.....KENT TAYLOR
___ON TOP OF OLD SMOKY ....COL .....1953.....GENE AUTRY
___PACK TRAIN ....COL .....1953.....GENE AUTRY

MARIN SAIS

___THE FIGHTING COWBOY ....SPR .....1933.....BUFFALO BILL, JR.
___WHEELS OF DESTINY ....UNI ......1934.....KEN MAYNARD
___RAWHIDE ROMANCE ....SUP .....1934.....BUFFALO BILL, JR.
___CIRCLE OF DEATH ....KEN .....1935.....MONTIE MONTANA
___TRAILING TROUBLE........................GN ....1937.....KEN MAYNARD
___PIONEER TRAIL ....COL .....1938.....JACK LUDEN
___PHANTOM GOLD ....COL .....1938.....JACK LUDEN
___RIDERS OF THE FRONTIER...........MON ....1939.....TEX RITTER
___WILD HORSE RANGE......................MON ....1940.....JACK RANDALL
___TWO GUN SHERIFF........................REP .....1941.....DON BARRY
___SADDLEMATES ....REP .....1941.....LIVINGSTON/STEELE
___BILLY THE KID IN SANTA FE ....PRC .....1941.....ROY ROGERS
___SIERRA SUE ....REP .....1941.....GENE AUTRY
___FRONTIER OUTLAWS ....PRC .....1944.....BUSTER CRABBE
___OATH OF VENGEANCE..................PRC .....1944.....BUSTER CRABBE
___BELLS OF ROSARITA.......................REP .....1945.....ROY ROGERS
___BORDER BADMEN ....PRC .....1945.....BUSTER CRABBE
___PRAIRIE RUSTLERS........................PRC .....1945.....BUSTER CRABBE
___LIGHTNING RAIDERS......................PRC .....1945.....BUSTER CRABBE
___TERRORS ON HORSEBACK ....PRC .....1946.....BUSTER CRABBE
___RIDE RYDER, RIDE...........................EL ....1949.....JIM BANNON
___ROLL THUNDER, ROLL ....EL ....1949.....JIM BANNON
___THE FIGHTING REDHEAD ....EL ....1949.....JIM BANNON
___THE COWBOY AND THE PRIZE .....EL ....1949.....JIM BANNON
FIGHTER

NANCY SAUNDERS

___SOUTH OF THE CHISHOLM TRAIL COL ..... 1947 ..... CHARLES STARRETT
___WEST OF DODGE CITY .... COL ..... 1947 ..... CHARLES STARRETT
___LAW OF THE CANYON .... COL ..... 1947 ..... CHARLES STARRETT
___PRAIRIE RAIDERS .... COL ..... 1947 ..... CHARLES STARRETT
___SIX GUN LAW .... COL ..... 1948 ..... CHARLES STARRETT
___WHIRLWIND RAIDERS .... COL ..... 1948 ..... CHARLES STARRETT
___OUTLAW COUNTRY .... WA .... 1949 ..... LASH LARUE
___ARIZONA TERRITORY .... MON .... 1950 ..... WHIP WILSON

ANN SAVAGE

___ARIZONA TRAIL .... UNI .... 1943 ..... TEX RITTER
___SADDLES AND SAGEBRUSH .... COL ..... 1943 ..... RUSSELL HAYDEN
___THE LAST HORSEMAN .... COL ..... 1944 ..... RUSSELL HAYDEN
___RENEGADE GIRL .... SG .... 1946 ..... ALAN CURTIS
___SATANS' CRADLE .... UA .... 1949 ..... DUNCAN RENALDO

VIRGINIA SAYLES (SALE)

___THE DUDE WRANGLER .... WW ...... 1930 ..... TOM KEENE
___SMOKE LIGHTNING .... FOX ..... 1933 ..... GEORGE O'BRIEN
___BLAZING THE WESTERN TRAIL .... COL ..... 1945 ..... CHARLES STARRETT
___BADMANS' TERRITORY .... RKO ..... 1946 ..... RANDOLPH SCOTT
___TRAIL STREET .... RKO ..... 1947 ..... RANDOLPH SCOTT

MARION SCHILLING

___THE SUNDOWN TRAIL .... RKO ..... 1931 ..... TOM KEENE
___A MANS' LAND .... ALL .... 1932 ..... HOOT GIBSON
___FIGHTING TO LIVE .... PRN ..... 1934 ..... REB RUSSELL
___THUNDER OVER TEXAS .... BEA ..... 1934 ..... GUINN WILLIAMS
___THE WESTERNER .... COL ..... 1934 ..... TIM McCOY
___STONE OF SILVER CREEK .... UNI .... 1935 ..... BUCK JONES
___GUNSMOKE ON THE GUADALUPE . KEN ..... 1935 ..... ROCKY CAMRON
___BLAZING GUNS .... KEN ..... 1935 ..... REB RUSSELL
___GUN PLAY (LUCKY BOOTS) .... BEA ..... 1935 ..... GUINN WILLIAMS
___RIO RATTLER .... REL ...... 1935 ..... TOM TYLER
___THE IDAHO KID .... COL ..... 1936 ..... REX BELL
___ROMANCE RIDES THE RANGE ..... SPE ..... 1936 ..... FRED SCOTT
___CAVALCADE OF THE WEST .... DIV .... 1936 ..... HOOT GIBSON

DOROTHY SEBASTIAN

___THE UTAH KID .... TIF .... 1930 ..... REX LEASE
___ROUGH RIDERS ROUNDUP .... REP ..... 1939 ..... ROY ROGERS
___THE ARIZONA KID .... REP ..... 1939 ..... ROY ROGERS
___KANSAS CYCLONE .... REP ..... 1941 ..... DON BARRY

HELEN SERVIS

___THE BIG SHOW ....REP ..... 1936 ..... GENE AUTRY
___GAY AMIGO ....UA .... 1949 ..... DUNCAN RENALDO
___DAUGHTER OF THE WEST ....FC .... 1949 ..... MARTHA VICKERS

ALMIRA SESSIONS

___THE BLAZING SUN ....COL ..... 1950 ..... GENE AUTRY
___THE OLD FRONTIER ....REP ..... 1950 ..... MONTE HALE
___WAGONS WEST ....MON .... 1952 ..... ROD CAMERON

BILLIE SEWARD

___LAW BEYOND THE RANGE ....COL ..... 1935 ..... TIM McCOY
___THE REVENGE RIDER ....COL ..... 1935 ..... TIM McCOY
___JUSTICE OF THE RANGE ....COL ..... 1935 ..... TIM McCOY
___RIDING WILD ....COL ..... 1935 ..... TIM McCOY
___BRANDED A COWARD ....SUP ..... 1935 ..... JOHNNY MACK BROWN
___TRAILS OF THE WILD ....AMB ..... 1935 ..... KERMIT MAYNARD
___THE MAN FROM GUNTOWN ....PUR ..... 1935 ..... TIM McCOY

JANET SHAW

___PRAIRIE THUNDER ....WB .... 1937 ..... DICK FORAN
___BAD MEN OF THUNDER GAP ....PRC ..... 1943 ..... NEWILL/O'BRIEN
___ARIZONA TRAIL ....UNI ...... 1943 ..... TEX RITTER

GLORIA SHEA

___THE DUDE BANDIT ....ALL ...... 1933 ..... HOOT GIBSON
___THE FIDDLIN' BUCKAROO ....UNI ...... 1933 ..... KEN MAYNARD
___SMOKING GUNS ....UNI ...... 1934 ..... KEN MAYNARD
___A DEMON FOR TROUBLE ....SUP ..... 1934 ..... BOB STEELE

KATHRYN SHELDON

___SUNSET TRAIL ....PAR ..... 1939 ..... WILLIAM BOYD
___SHOOTING HIGH ....20T ...... 1940 ..... GENE AUTRY
___ARIZONA BOUND ....MON .... 1941 ..... JONES/McCOY

ELAINE SHEPARD

___THE SINGING VAGABOND ....REP ..... 1935 ..... GENE AUTRY
___LAW OF THE RANGER ....COL ..... 1937 ..... BOB ALLEN
___THE FIGHTING TEXAN ....AMB ..... 1937 ..... KERMIT MAYNARD

ANN SHERIDAN

___HOME ON THE RANGE ....PAR ..... 1935 ..... RANDOLPH SCOTT
___RED BLOOD OF COURAGE ....AMB ..... 1935 ..... KERMIT MAYNARD
___ROCKY MOUNTAIN MYSTERY ....PAR ..... 1935 ..... RANDOLPH SCOTT

DOROTHY SHORT

___BROTHERS OF THE WEST ....VIC.......1937.....TOM TYLER
___HEART OF ARIZONA ....PAR .....1938.....WILLIAM BOYD
___WHERE THE BUFFALO ROAM ....MON ....1938.....TEX RITTER
___WILD HORSE CANYON ....MON ....1938.....JACK RANDALL
___CODE OF THE CACTUS ....VIC.......1939.....TIM McCOY
___THE SINGING COWGIRL.................GN ....1939.....DOROTHY PAGE
___PHANTOM RANCHER.......................COL .....1940.....KEN MAYNARD
___FRONTIER CRUSADER....................PRC .....1940.....TIM McCOY
___PONY POST ....UNI.......1940.....JOHNNY MACK BROWN
___TRAIL OF THE SILVER SPURS ......MON ....1941.....CORRIGAN/KING
___THE LONE RIDER FIGHTS BACK ..PRC .....1941.....GEORGE HOUSTON
___BULLETS FOR BANDITS ....COL .....1942.....ELLIOTT/RITTER

LOUISE STANLEY

___LAWLESS LAND ....REP .....1937.....JOHNNY MACK BROWN
___GUN LORDS OF STIRRUP BASIN..REP .....1937.....BOB STEELE
___SING COWBOY, SING ....GN ....1937.....TEX RITTER
___RIDERS OF THE ROCKIES ....GN ....1937.....TEX RITTER
___THUNDER IN THE DESERT ....REP .....1938.....BOB STEELE
___LAND OF FIGHTING MEN ....MON ....1938.....JACK RANDALL

Louise Stanley with Tex Ritter

___GUNSMOKE TRAIL ....MON .... 1938..... JACK RANDALL
___DURANGO VALLEY RAIDERS ....REP ..... 1938..... BOB STEELE
___GUN PACKER ....MON .... 1938..... JACK RANDALL
___YUKON FLIGHT ....MON .... 1940..... JIM NEWILL
___THE CHEYENNE KID ....MON .... 1940..... JACK RANDALL
___PINTO CANYON ....MET ..... 1940..... BOB STEELE
___LAND OF THE SIXGUNS ....MON .... 1940..... JACK RANDALL
___SKY BANDITS ....MON .... 1940..... JIM NEWILL
___WELLS FARGO DAYS.......................WB .... 1944..... DENNIS MOORE

PAT STARLING

___SAN FERNANDO VALLEY ....REP ..... 1944..... ROY ROGERS
___THE SINGING SHERIFF ....UNI ...... 1944..... BOB CROSBY
___RAINBOW OVER THE ROCKIES .... MON .... 1946..... JIMMY WAKELY
___FIGHTING MUSTANG ....AST...... 1948..... SUNSET CARSON
___DEADLINE ....AST...... 1948..... SUNSET CARSON
___SUNSET CARSON RIDES AGAIN .. AST...... 1948..... SUNSET CARSON
___BATTLING MARSHAL ....AST...... 1950..... SUNSET CARSON

ELEANOR STEWART

___HEADING FOR THE RIO GRANDE. GN .... 1936..... TEX RITTER
___ARIZONA DAYS ....GN .... 1937..... TEX RITTER

Eleanor Stewart with Jack Luden

___THE GUN RANGER .... REP ..... 1937 ..... BOB STEELE
___SANTA FE RIDES .... REL ...... 1937 ..... BOB CUSTER
___RANGE DEFENDERS .... REP ..... 1937 ..... LIVINGSTON/CORRIGAN
___THE RANGERS STEP IN .... COL ..... 1937 ..... BOB ALLEN
___WHERE TRAILS DIVIDE .... MON .... 1937 ..... TOM KEENE
___THE PAINTED TRAIL .... MON .... 1938 ..... TOM KEENE
___ROLLING CARAVANS .... COL ..... 1938 ..... JACK LUDEN
___STAGECOACH DAYS .... COL ..... 1938 ..... JACK LUDEN
___THE MEXICALI KID .... MON .... 1938 ..... JACK RANDALL
___FLAMING LEAD .... COL ..... 1939 ..... KEN MAYNARD
___PIRATES ON HORSEBACK .... PAR ..... 1941 ..... WILLIAM BOYD
___RIDERS OF THE TIMBERLINE .... PAR ..... 1941 ..... WILLIAM BOYD
___MYSTERY MAN .... UA .... 1944 ..... WILLIAM BOYD

PEGGY STEWART

___WELLS FARGO .... PAR ..... 1937 ..... JOEL McCREA
___TUCSON RAIDERS .... REP ..... 1944 ..... BILL ELLIOTT
___SILVER CITY KID .... REP ..... 1944 ..... ALLAN LANE
___STAGECOACH TO MONTEREY ..... REP ..... 1944 ..... ALLAN LANE
___CHEYENNE WILDCAT .... REP ..... 1944 ..... BILL ELLIOTT
___CODE OF THE PRAIRIE .... REP ..... 1944 ..... SUNSET CARSON
___FIREBRANDS OF ARIZONA .... REP ..... 1944 ..... SUNSET CARSON
___SHERIFF OF LAS VEGAS .... REP ..... 1944 ..... BILL ELLIOTT
___UTAH .... REP ..... 1945 ..... ROY ROGERS
___THE OREGON TRAIL .... REP ..... 1945 ..... SUNSET CARSON
___BANDITS OF THE BADLANDS .... REP ..... 1945 ..... SUNSET CARSON
___MARSHAL OF LAREDO .... REP ..... 1945 ..... BILL ELLIOTT
___ROUGH RIDERS OF CHEYENNE ... REP ..... 1945 ..... SUNSET CARSON
___CALIFORNIA GOLD RUSH .... REP ..... 1946 ..... BILL ELLIOTT
___DAYS OF BUFFALO BILL .... REP ..... 1946 ..... SUNSET CARSON
___ALIAS BILLY THE KID .... REP ..... 1946 ..... SUNSET CARSON
___RED RIVER RENEGADES .... REP ..... 1946 ..... SUNSET CARSON
___CONQUEST OF CHEYENNE .... REP ..... 1946 ..... BILL ELLIOTT
___SHERIFF OF REDWOOD VALLEY .. REP ..... 1946 ..... BILL ELLIOT
___STAGECOACH TO DENVER .... REP ..... 1946 ..... ALLAN LANE
___TRAIL TO SAN ANTONE .... REP ..... 1947 ..... GENE AUTRY
___VIGILANTES OF BOOMTOWN .... REP ..... 1947 ..... ALLAN LANE
___RUSTLERS OF DEVILS' CANYON . REP ..... 1947 ..... ALLAN LANE
___DEAD MANS' GOLD .... SG .... 1948 ..... LASH LARUE
___FRONTIER REVENGE .... SG .... 1948 ..... LASH LARUE
___RIDE RYDER, RIDE .... EL .... 1949 ..... JIM BANNON
___FIGHTING REDHEAD .... EL .... 1949 ..... JIM BANNON
___DESERT VIGILANTE .... COL ..... 1949 ..... CHARLES STARRETT
___THE BLACK LASH .... SG .... 1952 ..... LASH LARUE
___KANSAS TERRITORY .... MON .... 1952 ..... BILL ELLIOTT

___MONTANA INCIDENT .... MON ..... 1952..... WHIP WILSON
___SIX-GUN DECISION .... AA .... 1953..... GUY MADISON

Peggy Stewart with Sunset Carson

LINDA STIRLING

___SAN ANTONIO .... REP ..... 1944..... BILL ELLIOTT
___SHERIFF OF SUNDOWN .... REP ..... 1944..... ALLAN LANE
___VIGILANTES OF DODGE CITY .... REP ..... 1944..... BILL ELLIOTT
___THE TOPEKA TERROR .... REP ..... 1945..... ALLAN LANE
___SHERIFF OF CIMARRON .... REP ..... 1945..... SUNSET CARSON
___SANTA FE SADDLEMATES .... REP ..... 1945..... SUNSET CARSON
___THE CHEROKEE FLASH .... REP ..... 1945..... SUNSET CARSON
___WAGON WHEELS WESTWARD ..... REP ..... 1945..... BILL ELLIOTT
___RIO GRANDE RAIDERS .... REP ..... 1946..... SUNSET CARSON

PAULA STONE

___HOPALONG CASSIDY .... PAR ..... 1935..... WILLIAM BOYD
___TREACHERY RIDES THE RANGE . WB .... 1936..... DICK FORAN
___TRAILIN' WEST .... WB .... 1936..... DICK FORAN

Linda Stirling with Allan Lane, Eddie Parker, and George J. Lewis

JUNE STOREY

___HOME ON THE PRAIRIE .... REP ..... 1939 ..... GENE AUTRY
___BLUE MONTANA SKIES .... REP ..... 1939 ..... GENE AUTRY
___MOUNTAIN RHYTHM .... REP ..... 1939 ..... GENE AUTRY
___COLORADO SUNSET .... REP ..... 1939 ..... GENE AUTRY
___IN OLD MONTEREY .... REP ..... 1939 ..... GENE AUTRY
___SOUTH OF THE BORDER .... REP ..... 1939 ..... GENE AUTRY
___RANCHO GRANDE .... REP ..... 1940 ..... GENE AUTRY
___GAUCHO SERENADE .... REP ..... 1940 ..... GENE AUTRY
___CAROLINA MOON .... REP ..... 1940 ..... GENE AUTRY
___RIDE, TENDERFOOT, RIDE .... REP ..... 1940 ..... GENE AUTRY
___SONG OF THE PRAIRIE .... COL ..... 1945 ..... KEN CURTIS

GALE STORM

___SADDLEMATES .... REP ..... 1941 ..... LIVINGSTON/STEELE
___JESSE JAMES AT BAY .... REP ..... 1941 ..... ROY ROGERS
___RED RIVER VALLEY .... REP ..... 1941 ..... ROY ROGERS
___MAN FROM CHEYENNE .... REP ..... 1942 ..... ROY ROGERS
___FOREVER YOURS .... MON .... 1945 ..... JOHNNY MACK BROWN
___STAMPEDE .... MON .... 1949 ..... ROD CAMERON
___THE KID FROM TEXAS .... UNI .... 1950 ..... AUDIE MURPHY
___AL JENNINGS OF OKLAHOMA .... COL ..... 1951 ..... DAN DURYEA
___THE TEXAS RANGERS .... COL ..... 1951 ..... GEORGE MONTGOMERY

June Story with Gene Autry

GLORIA TALBOT

___DESERT PURSUIT .... MON .... 1952 ..... WAYNE MORRIS
___BORDER CITY RUSTLER .... AA .... 1953 ..... GUY MADISON
___NORTHERN PATROL .... MON .... 1953 ..... KIRBY GRANT

HELEN TALBOT

___CANYON CITY .... REP ..... 1943 ..... DON BARRY
___CALIFORNIA JOE .... REP ..... 1943 ..... DON BARRY
___OUTLAWS OF SANTA FE .... REP ..... 1944 ..... DON BARRY
___SONG OF NEVADA .... REP ..... 1944 ..... ROY ROGERS
___SAN FERNANDO VALLEY .... REP ..... 1944 ..... ROY ROGERS
___CORPUS CHRISTI BANDITS .... REP ..... 1945 ..... ALLAN LANE
___LONE TEXAS RANGER .... REP ..... 1945 ..... BILL ELLIOTT
___BELLS OF ROSARITA .... REP ..... 1945 ..... ROY ROGERS
___TRAIL OF KIT CARSON .... REP ..... 1945 ..... ALLAN LANE
___DON'T FENCE ME IN .... REP ..... 1945 ..... ROY ROGERS

EMMA TANSEY

___BEYOND THE RIO GRANDE .... BIL .... 1930 ..... JACK PERRIN
___THE GAMBLING TERROR .... REP ..... 1937 ..... JOHNNY MACK BROWN

___GUN LORDS OF STIRRUP BASIN .. REP ..... 1937 ..... BOB STEELE
___KNIGHT OF THE PLAINS .... SPE ..... 1938 ..... FRED SCOTT

RUTH TERRY

___CALL OF THE CANYON .... REP ..... 1942 ..... GENE AUTRY
___HEART OF THE GOLDEN WEST .... REP ..... 1942 ..... ROY ROGERS
___THE MAN FROM MUSIC MOUNTAIN .. REP ..... 1943 ..... ROY ROGERS
___HANDS ACROSS THE BORDER .... REP ..... 1944 ..... ROY ROGERS
___LAKE PLACID SERENADE .... REP ..... 1945 ..... ROY ROGERS

SHEILAH TERRY

___HAUNTED GOLD .... WB .... 1932 ..... JOHN WAYNE
___ROCKY RHODES .... UNI .... 1934 ..... BUCK JONES
___LAWLESS FRONTIER .... MON .... 1934 ..... JOHN WAYNE
___'NEATH ARIZONA SKIES .... MON .... 1934 ..... JOHN WAYNE

LYNN THOMAS

___COVERED WAGON RAID .... REP ..... 1950 ..... ALLAN LANE
___THE MISSOURIANS .... REP ..... 1950 ..... MONTE HALE
___RED RIVER SHORE .... REP ..... 1953 ..... REX ALLEN

CAROL THURSTON

___THE LAST ROUNDUP .... COL ..... 1947 ..... GENE AUTRY
___APACHE CHIEF .... LIP .... 1949 ..... ALAN CURTIS
___YUKON VENGEANCE .... AA .... 1954 ..... KIRBY GRANT

LUPITA TOVAR

___BORDER LAW .... COL ..... 1931 ..... BUCK JONES
___THE FIGHTING GRINGO .... RKO ..... 1939 ..... GEORGE O'BRIEN
___SOUTH OF THE BORDER .... REP ..... 1939 ..... GENE AUTRY
___TWO GUN SHERIFF .... REP ..... 1941 ..... DON BARRY
___GUN TO GUN .... WB .... 1944 ..... ROBERT SHAYNE

ROSA TURICH

___ROSE OF THE RIO GRANDE .... MON .... 1938 ..... JOHN CARROLL
___STARLIGHT OVER TEXAS .... MON .... 1938 ..... TEX RITTER
___SOUTH OF MONTEREY .... MON .... 1946 ..... GILBERT ROLAND
___RIDING THE CALIFORNIA TRAIL ... MON .... 1947 ..... GILBERT ROLAND
___SON OF BILLY THE KID .... SG .... 1949 ..... LASH LARUE
___PHANTOM STALLION .... REP ..... 1954 ..... REX ALLEN

MINERVA URECAL

___FRONTIER SCOUT .... GN .... 1938 ..... GEORGE HOUSTON
___THE SAGEBRUSH FAMILY TRAILS WEST . PRC ..... 1940 ..... BOBBY CLARK

___ARKANSAS JUDGE .... REP ..... 1941 ..... ROY ROGERS
___COWBOY AND THE BLONDE .... FOX ..... 1941 ..... GEORGE MONTGOMERY
___SONS OF THE PIONEERS .... REP ..... 1942 ..... ROY ROGERS
___RIDING THROUGH NEVADA .... COL ..... 1942 ..... CHARLES STARRETT
___WAGON TRACKS WEST .... REP ..... 1943 ..... BILL ELLIOTT
___WANDERER OF THE WASTELAND RKO ..... 1945 ..... JAMES WARREN
___RAINBOW OVER TEXAS .... REP ..... 1946 ..... ROY ROGERS
___SIOUX CITY SUE .... REP ..... 1946 ..... GENE AUTRY
___APACHE ROSE .... REP ..... 1947 ..... ROY ROGERS
___BOWERY BUCKAROOS .... MON .... 1947 ..... BOWERY BOYS
___SADDLE PALS .... REP ..... 1947 ..... GENE AUTRY
___MARSHAL OF AMARILLO .... REP ..... 1948 ..... ALLAN LANE
___SUNDOWN IN SANTA FE .... REP ..... 1948 ..... ALLAN LANE
___OUTCAST OF THE TRAIL .... REP ..... 1949 ..... MONTE HALE
___ARIZONA COWBOY .... REP ..... 1950 ..... REX ALLEN
___TEXANS NEVER CRY .... COL ..... 1951 ..... GENE AUTRY
___TWO-GUN MARSHAL .... UA .... 1953 ..... GUY MADISON

VIRGINIA VALE

___MARSHAL OF MESA CITY .... RKO ..... 1939 ..... GEORGE O'BRIEN
___LEGION OF THE LAWLESS .... RKO ..... 1940 ..... GEORGE O'BRIEN
___BULLET CODE .... RKO ..... 1940 ..... GEORGE O'BRIEN
___PRAIRIE LAW .... RKO ..... 1940 ..... GEORGE O'BRIEN
___STAGE TO CHINO .... RKO ..... 1940 ..... GEORGE O'BRIEN
___TRIPLE JUSTICE .... RKO ..... 1940 ..... GEORGE O'BRIEN
___ROBBERS OF THE RANGE .... RKO ..... 1941 ..... TIM HOLT

HELEN VALKIS

___THE CHEROKEE STRIP .... WB .... 1937 ..... DICK FORAN
___BLAZING SIXES .... WB .... 1937 ..... DICK FORAN
___THE OLD BARN DANCE .... REP ..... 1938 ..... GENE AUTRY

ALBERTA VAUGHN

___WILD HORSE .... ALL ...... 1931 ..... HOOT GIBSON
___DARING DANGER .... COL ..... 1932 ..... TIM McCOY
___RANDY RIDES ALONE .... MON .... 1934 ..... JOHN WAYNE
___LARAMIE KID .... REL ...... 1935 ..... TOM TYLER

DOROTHY VAUGHN

___ROBIN HOOD OF TEXAS .... REP ..... 1947 ..... GENE AUTRY
___TRAIL TO SAN ANTONE.................. REP ..... 1947 ..... GENE AUTRY
___SONG OF IDAHO............................. COL ..... 1948 ..... KIRBY GRANT
___HOME IN SAN ANTONE .... COL ..... 1949 ..... ROY ACUFF
___RIDER FROM TUCSON .... RKO ..... 1950 ..... TIM HOLT

EVELYN VENABLE

___NORTH OF NOME ....COL ..... 1936 ..... JACK HOLT
___THE FRONTIERSMAN ....PAR ..... 1938 ..... WILLIAM BOYD
___LUCKY CISCO KID ....20T .... 1940 ..... CESAR ROMERO

ELENA VERDUGO

___EL DORADO PASS ....COL ..... 1948 ..... CHARLES STARRETT
___THE BIG SOMBRERO ....COL ..... 1949 ..... GENE AUTRY
___SNOW DOG ....MON .... 1950 ..... KIRBY GRANT
___GENE AUTRY AND THE MOUNTIES .. COL ..... 1950 ..... GENE AUTRY
___THE MARKSMAN ....AA .... 1953 ..... WAYNE MORRIS

VICTORIA VINTON

___PALS OF THE PRAIRIE ....IMP ...... 1934 ..... BUFFALO BILL, JR.
___CHEYENNE TORNADO ....KEN ..... 1935 ..... REB RUSSELL
___AMBUSH VALLEY ....REL ...... 1936 ..... BOB CUSTER
___VENGEANCE OF RANNAH ....REL ...... 1936 ..... BOB CUSTER
___THE SINGING BUCKAROO ....SPE ..... 1937 ..... FRED SCOTT

JANET WALDO

___ONE MANS' LAW ....REP ..... 1940 ..... DON BARRY
___SILVER STALLION ....MON .... 1941 ..... SHARPE/MASON
___THE BANDIT TRAIL ....RKO ..... 1941 ..... TIM HOLT
___LAND OF THE OPEN RANGE ....RKO ..... 1942 ..... TIM HOLT

WENDY WALDRON

___OVER THE BORDER ....MON .... 1950 ..... JOHNNY MACK BROWN
___TRAIL GUIDE ....RKO ..... 1952 ..... TIM HOLT
___TRAIL OF THE ARROW ....MON .... 1952 ..... GUY MADISON

ETHEL WALES

___THE DUDE WRANGLER ....WW ...... 1930 ..... TOM KEENE
___UNDER MONTANA SKIES ....TIF .... 1930 ..... KENNETH HARLAN
___THE FIGHTING FOOL ....COL ..... 1932 ..... TIM McCOY
___A MAN'S LAND ....ALL ...... 1932 ..... HOOT GIBSON
___THE FIGHTING PARSON ....ALL ...... 1933 ..... HOOT GIBSON
___BAR 20 RIDES AGAIN ....PAR ..... 1935 ..... WILLIAM BOYD
___FRONTIER PONY EXPRESS ....REP ..... 1939 ..... ROY ROGERS
___IN OLD CALIENTE ....REP ..... 1939 ..... ROY ROGERS
___DAYS OF JESSE JAMES ....REP ..... 1939 ..... ROY ROGERS
___KNIGHTS OF THE RANGE ....PAR ..... 1940 ..... RUSSELL HAYDEN
___HIDDEN GOLD ....PAR ..... 1940 ..... WILLIAM BOYD
___YOUNG BILL HICKOK ....REP ..... 1940 ..... ROY ROGERS
___BORDER VIGILANTES ....PAR ..... 1941 ..... WILLIAM BOYD

___LUMBERJACK .... UA .... 1944 ..... WILLIAM BOYD
___IN OLD SACRAMENTO .... REP ..... 1946 ..... BILL ELLIOTT

CHERYL WALKER

___SHADOWS ON THE SAGE .... REP ..... 1942 ..... TYLER/STEELE
___RHYTHM ROUNDUP .... COL ..... 1945 ..... KEN CURTIS
___TRIAL OR TRIGGER .... WB .... 1944 ..... ROBERT SHAYNE

BERYLE WALLACE

___ROUGH RIDING RHYTHM .... AMB ..... 1937 ..... KERMIT MAYNARD
___ROMANCE OF THE ROCKIES .... MON .... 1937 ..... TOM KEENE
___SUNSET ON THE DESERT .... REP ..... 1942 ..... ROY ROGERS

LUANA WALTERS

___END OF THE TRAIL .... COL ..... 1932 ..... TIM McCOY
___THE FIGHTING TEXANS .... MON .... 1933 ..... REX BELL
___ACES AND EIGHTS.......................... PUR ..... 1936 ..... TIM McCOY
___RIDE 'EM COWBOY .... UNI ...... 1936 ..... BUCK JONES
___UNDER STRANGE FLAGS .... CRE ..... 1937 ..... TOM KEENE
___WHERE THE WEST BEGINS .... MON .... 1938 ..... JACK RANDALL
___MEXICALI ROSE .... REP ..... 1939 ..... GENE AUTRY

Luana Walters with Charles (Durango Kid) Starrett and Kenneth McDonald

___THE RETURN OF WILD BILL ....COL .....1940.....BILL ELLIOTT
___THE TULSA KID ....REP .....1940.....DON BARRY
___THE RANGE BUSTERS ....MON ....1940.....CORRIGAN/KING
___THE DURANGO KID ....COL .....1940.....CHARLES STARRETT
___THE KIDS' LAST RIDE ....MON ....1941.....CORRIGAN/KING
___ACROSS THE SIERRAS ....COL .....1941.....BILL ELLIOTT
___LAW OF THE WOLF ....ZI..........1941.....DENNIS MOORE
___ARIZONA BOUND............................MON ....1941.....JONES/McCOY
___ROAD AGENT ....UNI.......1941.....DICK FORAN
___THE LONE STAR VIGILANTES.......COL .....1942.....ELLIOTT/RITTER
___LAWLESS PLAINSMAN ....COL .....1942.....CHARLES STARRETT
___DOWN TEXAS WAY ....MON ....1942.....JONES/McCOY
___COME ON, DANGER........................RKO .....1942.....TIM HOLT
___THUNDERING HOOFS......................RKO .....1942.....TIM HOLT
___BAD MEN OF THE HILLS ....COL .....1942.....CHARLES STARRETT

RUTH WARREN

___HELLO TROUBLE ....COL .....1932.....BUCK JONES
___THE LAST TRAIL ....FOX .....1933.....GEORGE O'BRIEN
___FORLORN RIVER ....PAR .....1937.....BUSTER CRABBE
___THE CISCO KID AND THE LADY ....20T.......1940.....CESAR ROMERO
___KING OF THE WILD HORSES.........COL .....1947.....PRESTON FOSTER

TWINKLE WATTS

___MAN FROM THE RIO GRANDE ......REP .....1943.....DON BARRY
___CANYON CITY ....REP .....1943.....DON BARRY
___CALIFORNIA JOE ....REP .....1943.....DON BARRY
___OUTLAWS OF SANTA FE ....REP .....1944.....DON BARRY
___SILVER CITY KID ....REP .....1944.....ALLAN LANE
___STAGECOACH TO MONTERREY...REP .....1944.....ALLAN LANE
___SHERIFF OF SUNDOWN ....REP .....1944.....ALLAN LANE
___THE TOPEKA TERROR ....REP .....1945.....ALLAN LANE
___CORPUS CHRISTI BANDITS...........REP .....1945.....ALLAN LANE
___TRAIL OF KIT CARSON ....REP .....1945.....ALLAN LANE

BARBARA WEEKS

___TWO FISTED JUSTICE ....COL .....1931.....TOM TYLER
___WHITE EAGLE ....COL .....1932.....BUCK JONES
___FORBIDDEN TRAIL ....COL .....1932.....BUCK JONES
___RUSTY RIDES ALONE ....COL .....1933.....TIM McCOY
___THE SUNDOWN RIDER ....COL .....1933.....BUCK JONES
___TWO FISTED SHERIFF....................COL .....1937.....CHARLES STARRETT
___ONE MAN JUSTICE..........................COL .....1937.....CHARLES STARRETT
___THE OLD WYOMING TRAIL ....COL .....1937.....CHARLES STARRETT

Barbara Weeks with Buck Jones

MARION WELDON

___DODGE CITY TRAIL........................COL .....1936.....CHARLES STARRETT
___COLORADO KID..............................REP .....1937.....BOB STEELE
___THE FEUD MAKER..........................REP .....1938.....BOB STEELE
___KNIGHT OF THE PLAINS ....SPE .....1938.....FRED SCOTT
___DESERT PATROL...........................REP .....1938.....BOB STEELE

JACQUELINE WELLS (JULIE BISHOP)

___SQUARE SHOOTER ....COL .....1935.....TIM McCOY
___THE KANSAS TERRORS.................REP .....1939.....LIVINGSTON/RENALDO
___THE RANGER AND THE LADY ....REP .....1940.....ROY ROGERS
___YOUNG BILL HICKOK......................REP .....1940.....ROY ROGERS
___BACK IN THE SADDLE ....REP .....1941.....GENE AUTRY
___LAST OF THE RED MEN ....COL .....1947.....JON HALL
___DEPUTY MARSHAL ....LIP ....1949.....JON HALL

MARTHA WENTWORTH

___SANTA FE UPRISING ....REP .....1946.....ALLAN LANE
___STAGECOACH TO DENVER...........REP .....1946.....ALLAN LANE
___VIGILANTES OF BOOMTOWN........REP .....1947.....ALLAN LANE
___HOMESTEADERS OF PARADISE ..REP .....1947.....ALLAN LANE
VALLEY

___OREGON TRAIL SCOUTS .... REP ..... 1947 ..... ALLAN LANE
___RUSTLERS OF DEVILS' CANYON . REP ..... 1947 ..... ALLAN LANE
___MARSHAL OF CRIPPLE CREEK ..... REP ..... 1947 ..... ALLAN LANE

HELEN WESTCOTT

___THUNDER OVER TEXAS .... BEA ..... 1934 ..... GUINN WILLIAMS
___BATTLES OF CHIEF PONTIAC .... MON .... 1952 ..... LEX BARKER
___GUN BELT .... UA .... 1953 ..... GEORGE MONTGOMERY

CLAIRE WHITNEY

___CHIP OF THE FLYING U .... UNI .... 1939 ..... JOHNNY MACK BROWN
___THE SILVER BULLET .... UNI .... 1942 ..... JOHNNY MACK BROWN
___THE HAUNTED MINE .... MON .... 1946 ..... JOHNNY MACK BROWN
___OKLAHOMA BADLANDS .... REP ..... 1948 ..... ALLAN LANE
___COWBOY CAVALIER .... MON .... 1948 ..... JIMMY WAKELY
___FRONTIER MARSHAL .... REP ..... 1949 ..... ALLAN LANE
___ROARING WESTWARD .... MON .... 1949 ..... JIMMY WAKELY

LOIS WILDE

___CARYL OF THE MOUNTAINS .... REL ...... 1936 ..... RIN TIN TIN
___THE SINGING COWBOY .... REP ..... 1936 ..... GENE AUTRY
___WILDCAT TROOPER .... AMB ..... 1936 ..... KERMIT MAYNARD
___STORMY TRAILS .... COL ..... 1936 ..... REX BELL
___BROTHERS OF THE WEST .... VIC .... 1937 ..... TOM TYLER
___HOPALONG RIDES AGAIN .... PAR ..... 1937 ..... WILLIAM BOYD
___DANGER VALLEY .... MON .... 1937 ..... JACK RANDALL

JAN WILEY

___TONTO BASIN OUTLAWS .... MON .... 1941 ..... CORRIGAN/KING
___THUNDER RIVER FEUD .... MON .... 1942 ..... CORRIGAN/KING
___DAWN ON THE GREAT DIVIDE ...... MON .... 1942 ..... BUCK JONES
___LAW MEN .... MON .... 1944 ..... JOHNNY MACK BROWN
___CISCO KID RETURNS .... MON .... 1945 ..... DUNCAN RENALDO

MARIE WINDSOR

___HELLFIRE .... REP ..... 1949 ..... BILL ELLIOTT
___THE SHOWDOWN .... REP ..... 1950 ..... BILL ELLIOTT
___DAKOTA LIL .... FOX ..... 1950 ..... GEORGE MONTGOMERY
___OUTLAW WOMEN .... HOW .... 1952 ..... MARIE WINDSOR

ISABEL WITHERS

___LAW MEN .... MON .... 1944 ..... JOHNNY MACK BROWN
___WILD BEAUTY .... UNI .... 1946 ..... DON PORTER
___RIDERS IN THE SKY .... COL ..... 1949 ..... GENE AUTRY

HARLENE WOOD

___THE LAW RIDES .... SUP ..... 1936 ..... BOB STEELE
___LAW AND LEAD .... COL ..... 1936 ..... REX BELL
___VALLEY OF TERROR .... AMB ..... 1937 ..... KERMIT MAYNARD
___FEUD OF THE TRAIL .... VIC .... 1937 ..... TOM TYLER
___WHISTLING BULLETS .... AMB ..... 1937 ..... KERMIT MAYNARD
___BORDER PHANTOM .... REP ..... 1937 ..... BOB STEELE

JOAN WOODBURY

___THE EAGLES' BROOD .... PAR ..... 1935 ..... WILLIAM BOYD
___BULLDOG COURAGE .... PUR ..... 1935 ..... TIM McCOY
___THE LIONS' DEN .... PUR ..... 1936 ..... TIM McCOY
___SONG OF THE GRINGO .... GN .... 1936 ..... TEX RITTER
___IN OLD CHEYENNE .... REP ..... 1941 ..... ROY ROGERS
___RIDE ON VAQUERO .... 20T ...... 1941 ..... CESAR ROMERO
___SUNSET SERENADE .... REP ..... 1942 ..... ROY ROGERS
___FLAME OF THE WEST .... MON .... 1945 ..... JOHNNY MACK BROWN
___NORTHWEST TRAIL .... SG .... 1945 ..... BOB STEELE

BARBARA WOODELL

___I SHOT BILLY THE KID .... LIP .... 1950 ..... DON BARRY
___CANYON RAIDERS .... MON .... 1951 ..... WHIP WILSON
___FORT OSAGE .... MON .... 1952 ..... ROD CAMERON
___MONTANA INCIDENT .... MON .... 1952 ..... WHIP WILSON

CONSTANCE WORTH

___CYCLONE ON HORSEBACK .... RKO ..... 1941 ..... TIM HOLT
___KANSAS CYCLONE .... REP ..... 1941 ..... DON BARRY
___CYCLONE PRAIRIE RANGERS ...... COL ..... 1944 ..... CHARLES STARRETT
___SAGEBRUSH HEROES .... COL ..... 1945 ..... CHARLES STARRETT
___WESTERN RENEGADES .... MON .... 1949 ..... JOHNNY MACK BROWN

WEN WRIGHT

___TRAIL TO GUNSIGHT .... UNI ...... 1944 ..... EDDIE DEW
___THE WHISPERING SKULL .... PRC ..... 1944 ..... THE TEXAS RANGERS
___GUNSMOKE .... MON .... 1945 ..... JOHNNY MACK BROWN
___MARKED FOR MURDER .... PRC ..... 1945 ..... TEX RITTER

___CALIFORNIA GOLD RUSH ....REP .....1946.....BILL ELLIOTT

MARIS WRIXON

___SUNSET IN WYOMING ....REP .....1941.....GENE AUTRY
___SONS OF THE PIONEERS ....REP .....1942.....ROY ROGERS
___TRAIL TO GUNSIGHT ....UNI.......1944.....EDDIE DEW

JANE WYATT

___HURRICANE SMITH ....REP .....1941.....RAY MIDDLETON
___BUCKSKIN FRONTIER ....UA........1943.....RICHARD DIX
___THE KANSAN ....UA........1943.....RICHARD DIX

PEGGY WYNNE

___WILD COUNTRY ....PRC .....1947.....EDDIE DEAN
___TRAILING DANGER ....MON ....1947.....JOHNNY MACK BROWN
___DESPERADOES OF DODGE CITY .REP .....1948.....ALLAN LANE
___THE DENVER KID ....REP .....1948.....ALLAN LANE

CHARLOTTE WYNTERS

___IVORY HANDLED GUN ....UNI.......1935.....BUCK JONES
___SUNSET TRAIL ....PAR .....1939.....WILLIAM BOYD
___RENEGADE TRAIL ....PAR .....1939.....WILLIAM BOYD

CLARA KIMBALL YOUNG

___THREE ON A TRAIL ....PAR .....1936.....WILLIAM BOYD
___OH SUSANNA ....REP .....1936.....GENE AUTRY
___HILLS OF OLD WYOMING...............PAR .....1937.....WILLIAM BOYD
___THE FRONTIERSMAN ....PAR .....1938.....WILLIAM BOYD

POLLY ANN YOUNG

___THE ONE WAY TRAIL.......................COL .....1931.....TIM McCOY
___THE MAN FROM UTAH....................MON ....1934.....JOHN WAYNE
___THE CRIMSON TRAIL.......................UNI........1935.....BUCK JONES
___HIS FIGHTING BLOOD ....AMB .....1935.....KERMIT MAYNARD
___THE BORDER PATROLMAN ....FOX .....1936.....GEORGE O'BRIEN
___WOLF CALL ....MON ....1939.....JOHN CARROLL
___MURDER ON THE YUKON ....MON ....1940.....JIM NEWILL

KEY TO STUDIO ABBREVIATIONS

AA ....Allied Artists
ACT ......Action Pictures
AJA ......Ajax
ALL.......Allied
AMB .....Ambassador
AME .....American Pictures Corp.
ARG .....Argosy
ART ......Artclass
AST ......Astor
ATL ......Atlantic
AYW .....Aywon

BEA ......Beaumont
BFD ......Beacon First Division
B4.........Big Four
BIL........Biltmore Productions

CLY ......Colony
COL......Columbia
COM .....Commodore
COS .....Cosmos
CRE .....Crescent

DIV ....Diversion

EL.........Eagle Lion
EMP .....Empire

FC ....Film Classics
FD ....First Division
FE.........Film Enterprises
FM ....Freuler/Monarch
FN ....First National
FOX......Fox Film Corp.
FRA ......Fraser Productions

GN ....Grand National

HOF .....J. H. Hoffberg
HOW ....Howco Productions
HP ....Robert J. Horner Prod.

IMP.......Imperial

KEN......Kent

LIP ....Lippert

MAJ ......Majestic
MAS .....Mascot
MET .....Metropolitan
MGM ....Metro, Goldwyn, Mayer
MON .....Monogram

PAR......Paramount
PRC .....Producers Releasing Corp.
PRN .....Principal Attraction
PUR .....Puritan

RAY......Rayton Talking Pictures/
.... Precido
REL ......Reliable/Wm. Steiner
REP ......Republic
RES ......Resolute
RKO .....Radio Keith Orpheum Corp.
RP ....Roundup Pictures

S & S ....Stage and Screen
SEC ......Security
SG ....Screen Guild
SPE ......Spectrum
SPR......Superior Talking Pictures
SUP ......Supreme/Wm. Steiner
SYN ......Syndicate

TIF ....Tiffany
20T ....20th Century Fox

UA ....United Artists
UNI ....Universal

VIC ....Victory

WA ....Western Adventure
WB ....Warner Bros.
WW ......KBS/World Wide

ZI ....Arthur Ziehn Productions

ABOUT THE AUTHORS

STEVE TURNER

Born in Morganton, North Carolina, Steve Turner was raised in Richmond, Virginia. He has lived in Charlotte, North Carolina for the past 30 years. After graduating from Benedictine High School in Richmond, he attended Guilford College near Greensboro, earning his degree in 1958. Following a stint in the United States Army, Turner entered the insurance business with the General Adjustment Bureau, Inc. and is currently a Senior Casualty Underwriter for the Hartford Insurance Group. He is married, has two daughters and a grandson.

Growing up in Richmond he attended the Grand Theatre nearly every Saturday to see his cowboy heroes. Tom Tyler and John Wayne were his favorites. He looked forward to visiting his grandparents in Morganton where he would frequent the Alva and Mimosa Theatres to see "B" westerns.

EDGAR M. WYATT

A native of Raleigh, North Carolina, Edgar Marshall Wyatt retired as president of the family business, Wyatt-Quarles Seed Company, at the close of 1986 after 48 years in the organization. He is a graduate of Wake Forest University and served in the 63rd Infantry in the European theatre during World War II. He and his wife Bebe have three children and three grandchildren.

As a boy Wyatt spent many Saturday afternoons at the Capitol, Superba or Palace Theatres cheering for his cowboys, and yes, cowgirls. Interest in Western films and in the players who made them was rekindled several years ago and since that time he has written two self-published biographies, *More Than a Cowboy*, the life and Films of Fred Thomson and Silver King, *The Hoxie Boys*, the lives and Films of Jack and Al Hoxie, and*ABCs of Movie Cowboys*.

Other Movie / TV Books Available from Empire Publishing:

100 Best Films of the Century by Barry Norman
1001 Toughest TV Trivia Questions of All Time by Vincent Terrace
Allan "Rocky" Lane, Republic's Action Ace by Chuck Thornton and David Rothel
America on the Rerun by David Story
An Ambush of Ghosts by David Rothel
Bad Guys by Williams K. Everson
Black Hollywood by Gary Null
Bugsy by James Toback
Candid Cowboys, Vols. 1 & 2 by Neil Summers
Classic TV Westerns by Ronald Jackson
Classics of the Gangster Film by Robert Bookbinder
Classics of the Horror Film by Williams K. Everson
Complete Films of Bela Lugosi by Richard Bojarski
Complete Films of Bette Davis by Gene Ringgold
Complete Films of Cary Grant by Donald Deschner
Complete Films of Cecil B. DeMille by Gene Ringgold and DeWitt Bodeen
Complete Films of Charlie Chaplin by Gerald D. McDonald
Complete Films of Clark Gable by Gabe Essoe
Complete Films of Edward G. Robinson by Alvin H. Marill
Complete Films of Erroll Flynn by Tony Thomas, et al
Complete Films of Frank Capra by Victor Scherle & William Turner Levy
Complete Films of Gary Cooper by Homer Dickens
Complete Films of Henry Fonda by Tony Thomas
Complete Films of Ingrid Bergman by Lawrence J. Quirk
Complete Films of James Cagney by Homer C. Dickens
Complete Films of Jeanette MacDonald and Nelson Eddy by Philip Castanza
Complete Films of Joan Crawford by Lawrence J. Quirk
Complete Films of John Huston by John McCarty
Complete Films of John Wayne by Mark Ricci, et al
Complete Films of Judy Garland by Joe Morella and Edward Z Epstein
Complete Films of Laurel & Hardy by William K. Everson
Complete Films of Mae West by Jon Tuska
Complete Films of Marilyn Monroe by Michael Conway and Mark Ricci
Complete Films of Marlene Dietrich by Homer Dickens
Complete Films of Orson Wells by James Howard
Complete Films of Rita Hayworth by Gene Ringgold
Complete Films of Spencer Tracy by Donald Deschner
Complete Films of Steve McQueen by Casey St. Chamez
Complete Films of the Marx Brothers by Allen Eyles
Complete Films of W. C. Fields by Donald Deschner
Complete Films of William Holden by Lawrence J. Quirk
Complete Films of William Powell by Lawrence J. Quirk
Cult Horror Films by Everman
Curly by Joan Howard Maurer
Dick Tracy: America's Most Famous Detective edited by Bill Crouch, Jr.
Divine Images by Roy Kinnard and Tim Davis
Don Miller's Hollwood Corral by Smith & Hulse
Early Classics of the Foreign Film by Parker Tyler
Feature Players: The Stories Behind the Faces, Vol. 2 by Jim & Tom Goldrup
Film Flubs by Bill Givens
Films and Career of Elvis by Steven Zmijewsky and Boris Zmijewski
Films Flubs, The Sequal by Bill Givens
Films of Alan Ladd by Marilyn Henry and Ron DeSourdis
Films of Alfred Hitchcock by Robert A. Harris and Michael S. Lasky
Films of Arnold Schwarzenegger by John L. Flynn
Films of Brigitte Bardot by Crawley

Films of Carole Lombard by Fred W. Ott
Films of Charles Bronson by Jerry Vermilye
Films of Clint Eastwood by Boris Zmijewsky and Lee Pfeiffer
Films of Dustin Hoffman by Douglas Brode
Films of Elizabeth Taylor by Jerry Vermilye and Aldo Vigano
Films of Frank Sinatra by Gene Ringgold and Clifford McCarty
Films of Gina Lollobrigida by Maurizio Ponzi
Films of Gloria Swanson by Lawrence J. Quirk
Films of Gregory Peck by John Griggs
Films of Greta Garbo by Conway et al
Films of Hopalong Cassidy by Francis M. Nevins, Jr.
Films of Jack Nicholson by Douglas Brode
Films of Jane Fonda by George Hadley-Garcia
Films of Katharine Hepburn by Homer Dickens
Films of Kirk Douglas by Tony Thomas
Films of Lauren Bacall by Lawrence J. Quirk
Films of Laurence Olivier by Margaret Morley
Films of Marlon Brando by Tony Thomas
Films of Norma Shearer by Jack Jacobs and Myron Braum
Films of Olivia DeHavilland by Tony Thomas
Films of Paul Newman by Lawrence J. Quirk
Films of Peter Lorre by Stephen D. Youngkin, James Bigwood, and Raymond Cabana, Jr.
Films of Robert DeNiro by Douglas Brode
Films of Robert Redford by James Spada
Films of Sean Connery by Lee Pfeiffer and Phillip Lisa
Films of Shirley MacLaine by Christopher Paul Denis
Films of Shirley Temple by Robert Windeler
Films of the Bowery Boys by David Hayes and Brent Walker
Films of the Eighties by Douglas Brode
Films of the Fifties by Douglas Brode
Films of the Forties by Tony Thomas
Films of the Seventies by Robert Bookbinder
Films of the Sixties by Douglas Brode
Films of the Thirties by Jerry Vermilye
Films of the Twenties by Jerry Vermilye
Films of Warren Beatty by Lawrence Quirk
Films of Woody Allen by Douglas Brode
Final Curtain: Deaths of Noted Movie & TV Personalities
First Films by Jami Bernard
Frankly, My Dear by Bloch
Garth Brooks Scrapbook by Lee Randall
Gene Autry Reference-Trivia-Scrapbook by David Rothel
Gilligan, Maynard and Me by Bob Denver
Great Baseball Films by Rob Edelman
Great French Films by James Reid Paris
Great German Films by Frederick W. Ott
Great Italian Films by Jerry Vermilye
Great Science Fiction Films by Richard Meyers
Hello, I Must Be Going by Chandler
Hispanic Hollywood by George Hadley-Garcia
Hollywood Cheesecake by Madison S. Lacy and Don Morgan
Hollywood Musical by Tony Thomas
Hollywood Western by William K. Everson
Hollywood's Hollywood by Rudy Behlmer & Tony Thomas
Howard Hughes in Hollywood by Tony Thomas
Incredible World of 007 by Lee Pfeiffer & Philip Lisa

Jack Lemmon: His Films and Career by Joe Baltake
James Dean: Behind the Scene by Adams & Burns, ed.
Jewish Image in American Film by Lester D. Friedman
Joel McCrea, Riding the High Country by Tony Thomas
John Wayne Scrapbook by Lee Pfeiffer
King Cowboy: Tom Mix and the Movies by Robert S. Birchard
Life & Films of Buck Jones: The Silent Era by Buck Rainey
Life & Films of Buck Jones: The Sound Era by Buck Rainey
Lost Films of the Fifties by Douglas Brode
Madonna Scrapbook by Lee Randall
Modern Horror Film by John McCarty
Moe Howard & the Three Stooges by Moe Howard
More Character People by Arthur F. McClure, Alfred E. Twomey, & Ken Jones
More Classics of the Horror Film by William K. Everson
More Cowboy Shooting Stars by John A. Rutherford and Richard B. Smith, III
More Films of the Thirties by Jerry Vermilye
Movie Psychos and Madmen by John McCarty
Nightmare Never Ends: The Official History of Freddy Krueger by William Schoell
Northern Exposure Book: The Official Publication of the Television of the Television Series by Louis Chunovic
Official Andy Griffith Show Scrapbook by Lee Pfeiffer
Official John Wayne Reference Book by Charles John Kieskalt
Official TV Western Book, Vols. 1, 2,3, & 4 by Neil Summers
Quantum Leap Book: The Official Publication of the Television Series by Louis Chunovic
Randolph Scott / A Film Biography by Jefferson Brim Crow, III
Republic Confidential: Volume2 - The Players by Jack Mathis
Roy Rogers Reference-Trivia-Scrapbook by David Rothel
Saddle Pals by Garv Towell and Wayne E. Keates
Second Feature by John Cocchi
Sherlock Holmes by Chris Steinbrunner & Norman Michaels
Sinatra Scrapbook by Gary L. Doctor
Son of Film Flubs by Bill Givens
The "Cheers" Trivia Book by Mark Wenger
The Cowboy and the Kid by J. Brim Crow III and Jack H. Smith
The Cutting Room Floor by Laurent Bouzereau
The Dick Powell Story by Tony Thomas
The Real Bob Steele and a Man Called Brad by Bob Nareau
They Sang! They Danced! They Romanced! by John Springer
This is Hollyood by Ken Schessler
Those Fabulous Serial Heroines by Buck Rainey
Those Great Cowboy Sidekicks by David Rothel
Three Stooges Scrapbook by Jeff Lenburg, Joan Howard Maurer, Greg Lenburg
Thrillers: Seven Decades of Classic Film Suspense by John McCarthy
Tim Holt by David Rothel
Tom Mix Book by M. G. "Bud" Norris
Tom Mix Highlights by Andy Woytowch
West That Never Was by Tony Thomas
Western Films of John Ford by J. A. Place
Whatever Happened to Randolph Scott? by C. H. Scott
When Hollywood Was Fun: Snapshots of an Era by Gene Lester and Peter Laufer
Who Is That? by Warren B. Meyers
Wonderful Life: The Films and Career of James Stewart by Tony Thomas
Words and Shadows by Jim Hitt
You Ain't Heard Nothin' Yet by John P. Fennell